DECEIT

DECEIT

A TRUE STORY OF DOMESTIC INFIDELITY AND BETRAYAL WITH SALACIOUS DETAILS RECORDED BY WIRETAP

VERNON BAUMRIND

© Vernon Baumrind

Deceit
Copyright © 2023 Vernon Baumrind. All rights reserved.

All rights reserved. No part of this publication may be reproduced, distributed, or transmitted in any form or by any means, including photocopying, recording, or other electronic or mechanical methods, without the prior written permission of the publisher, except in the case of brief quotations embodied in critical reviews and certain other noncommercial uses permitted by copyright law.

ISBN: 979-8-88759-803-1 (paperback)
ISBN: 979-8-88759-804-8 (ebook)

DEDICATION

To my two children who have always been and will forever be at the center of my heart and soul; and to Jan L. Warner and Robert C. Schnackenberg for whom I will always be eternally grateful for their expertise and professionalism in the efforts put forth to benefit the children and the outcome of this story.

PREFACE

Although I've always understood one should not start a communication with an apology, I am uneasy about undertaking exposure of such sensitive subjects as related herein. However, as I began to recount this personal experience, by breathing life into words, I did so with the hope that in some small way this chronicle would reveal valuable life lessons.

The theme of this true-life story - marital infidelity and its effect on the families of those who are touched by it—is an age-old issue that has been repeated ad nauseum throughout human history, more than we'd like to admit. However, this account is unique in part because the two antagonists' intimate conversations at critical stages of the narrative are captured in recordable form made possible by a telephone landline wiretap. This story could only have occurred prior to the advent of cell phone technology in the late 1980s, since it is not practical today to tap a cell phone. The action taken to counteract the deeds of the two antagonists was done at the risk of violating federal wiretapping statutes with serious negative consequences. This story of marital espionage gained national acclaim due to the legal precedent of the case and the publicity that resulted from nation-wide news coverage of the legalities, including the airing of the story on a segment of ABC's 20/20 program in 1985.

These events happened forty-five years ago. So, why wait so long to reveal it? The two children who were the focus and purpose of the effort put forth in this narrative would likely have been affected detrimentally by the salacious content in a publication of the recordings during the early years of their lives. In fact, the family court judge sealed the file, including the tapes and the transcriptions of those tapes, for the protection of the children after legal proceedings in 1979. For this reason, only now is the complete story being revealed.

There is much to learn from this story, but in the end, it serves to remind us that out of bad, can come good. Ultimately, I hope this book is inspirational and changes lives for the better.

ACKNOWLEDGEMENT

I sincerely appreciate the contributions made to the writing of this story by my good friend and business associate, Bruce Whitney, who provided insightful analysis to the recurring conceptual themes throughout the narration of this story, as well as editing improvements. Metaphorically, if I go into any battle, I want Bruce on my side, as he has been on more than just this occasion.

I am immensely appreciative of my children who not only were the source of my strength to pull off the miracle accomplished in this story; but, much more so, for the caliber of people they are today; exemplifying everything that is good in humanity—thus, validating the extraordinary efforts put forth to assure that they had the very best chance of succeeding and flourishing in every aspect of life as the well-grounded parents and citizens they have become.

CHAPTER ONE

It was December 6, 1978, a sunny Wednesday afternoon, and I was pushing my children on the swing in our backyard, back and forth, back and forth. My son, David, almost five, and my two-and-a-half-year-old daughter, Jade, giggled with joy, unaware of the thoughts that tortured me. I had been scorned and rebuffed for weeks by my wife for reasons I did not understand. It suddenly came to me like the final piece in a puzzle, as if someone had handed me a note, or whispered it in my ear. Ewing was screwing my wife. Dr. James Ewing, Linda's gynecologist, the man who had delivered our youngest child, Jade, was screwing her. Ewing! Of course!

"Stupid," I scolded myself for not suspecting this earlier. Four days earlier, Linda had told me she didn't love me any longer, that we should separate, and that she wanted me to move immediately to the empty bedroom upstairs next to David's. I had been miserable because of her shocking pronouncement and rejection of me, and now, with this revelation, I was furious at myself for being so oblivious. I had fallen out of favor and was being discarded, cast out! Someone new had come along. Her doctor was far more appealing and provided new excitement. As I pushed the swing, this sudden insight had me feeling as though my skin had burst into flames, as if frenzy had become my blood. A sickening, expanding sourness and gnawing desperation took over my stomach.

Woefully in love with her almost from the moment I had met her thirteen years prior, I was now in excruciating emotional pain that I could feel on a physical level. This revelation explained everything. I now understood the cold, calloused and indifferent treatment I'd been getting from her for several months, the details of which would unravel shortly. It now made sense to me why Linda had asked me weeks prior to start coming home from work early on Wednesday afternoons to take care of the children while she went "shopping." I recalled times in previous weeks when I would come home and find her quickly hanging up the phone.

I reflected to October and November. Having no idea then what had gone wrong in our lives, not knowing why she was treating me so indifferently, I kept trying to get her to discuss her issues with me, but she refused to admit any. Weeks later when her demeanor was no different and I brought up the topic again, she insisted nothing was wrong, that she didn't want to discuss it, and she walked away. When I suggested marriage counseling, she replied that it was a ridiculous idea and waste of money, but I persevered, and finally, just before Thanksgiving, she agreed. We went three times together, with the counselor meeting with us separately. I was in love with her, and, when asked by the counselor, I told him I loved my wife.

I thought the sessions were productive and even felt a little resurgence of the relationship, but then, without explanation, Linda refused to go back. She erected that same barrier which I had sought counseling to overcome. I didn't learn until months later that the counselor had learned about her relationship with Ewing. Apparently, she had been honest with him, but professional ethics would not permit him to tell me what he knew. With the counselor now aware of the affair and with her not willing to give up the relationship with Ewing, she did not have a reason to continue the counseling sessions. She had become insensitive and indifferent to what we had together and no longer had any interest in our marriage. So entrenched was she in her behavior that nothing I said or did would move her. Her mind was made up. She was not returning to counseling. I didn't know this at the time, though, and to no advantage, I attended one last session alone, at which time the counselor told me there was no reason for me to continue and that I should seek legal advice.

Initially, I was unsuspecting. I only knew she no longer loved me. Then, she asked that I keep the children on Wednesday afternoons. "Going shopping," she had said. Pretenses! Bold-faced lies! Now, it all made sense.

Ewing and his wife and two children moved into our neighborhood shortly after Jade was born. We became friends. Soon after, he and his wife, Louise, and Linda started taking evening walks around the neighborhood. I remained at home with the children to get their bedtime activities started.

When the truth dawned on me that Wednesday afternoon in December in our backyard, I told the children to stay where they were as I gave them one last push in the swing. I was hoping I could dash into the house and return to them before the swing slowed to a stop. I bolted for the house, racing through the downstairs directly to the master bathroom. In my throat I could feel a cry of "Linda, God, no." I reached above the sink to the mirrored cabinet door and opened it, preparing myself for what I suspected I would discover. Her diaphragm case was there, the diaphragm Dr.

Ewing had prescribed for her. The case was empty. Gone, I realized, for their exclusive use. The sudden elucidation of the truth left me sick with despair, disgust, and anger.

It was Christmastime and we had planned to decorate the tree that night, but everything had changed. With the revelation, I now saw a different wife—a lying, cheating, deceiving adulterous wife. How was I supposed to act as if nothing had changed? *Everything had changed.* My thoughts were suddenly interrupted as my daughter appeared at my feet. "Daddy," she cried. As I looked down at her I knew—yes, everything had changed.

I knew where they were, the two of them: his office. He didn't work on Wednesdays. I knew his office was closed to patients on Wednesday afternoons. I grabbed the children and raced to the car, put them in their car seats, buckled them in, and backed out the driveway and down Pinckney Avenue en route to his office uptown, not knowing for sure what I was going to do, but beginning to realize what I must do.

It was after four o'clock and the sky had already begun to darken. It seemed as if winter had turned everything cold and dead. They had already had several hours together. How many Wednesdays had I conveniently been their babysitter while they carried on this affair? How long had this been going on?

I just needed to catch them together; to confirm what I already knew in my heart. But, by now they might have already gone their separate ways. And, as it was, catching them may not have been the best thing to do - except for the opportunity to confirm my suspicions. I would need to keep this knowledge to myself for now. I pulled into the Holiday Inn parking lot, across an expanse of concrete between the motel and his office building and parked between cars to conceal my presence. The children were content in their car seats. I was a wreck! Sick at heart and mad as hell, feeling every emotion within the whole spectrum of human emotions. Now it all made sense.

I had two young children in the back seat who might get impatient at any moment, making things more difficult, but luck was with me and, thankfully, the wait was short. There she was, the mother of my children, with another man's semen in her. She was walking down the steel stairwell from the second floor at the back of his four-story medical building, having completed her afternoon rendezvous with this son of a bitch I wanted to tear into and kill. Even now, I can't explain why my wrath was not directed toward her, but that was not my immediate thought. My animosity was directed at him.

The children are all I have left, I thought. But I knew the likelihood of a father gaining custody of two small children was remote, and I was fearful of losing them in a custody battle that was certain to lie ahead. Taking one look back at the two innocent children, happy in their car seats, feeling the profound love I had for them, I knew now what I had to do, even with the overwhelming legal disadvantage I faced. My only chance of getting custody of these two little ones would be to control my emotions and contain my impulses. I could not do anything rash. I could not raise Ewing's or Linda's suspicions that I knew what was going on. This knowledge would have to be mine alone for the time. They would have to continue feeling secure in their illicit relationship, meaning I could not confront them. I could not tear into that bastard, as I felt inclined to do. Against all odds, I would have to outwit and outmaneuver them.

This was going to be the fight of my life. I would have to hold everything in and hope I could do this long enough to gather evidence of their affair hoping to gain some advantage in an inevitable custody battle ahead. If I did otherwise, all would be lost. That was the supreme challenge at the time. I didn't know what it would take to get custody. While I figured that out, I would need to give them time and opportunity to be as bad as they could be on their own as if undetected. I had no idea how long it would take to get enough evidence, but I knew it was necessary for me to go along with what was happening. Without evidence, I would lose my children and I could not fathom giving them up to Jimmy Ewing as their full-time parent. That could not happen. My love for my children and the fear of losing them was the source of my strength.

We knew Jimmy Ewing was a derelict father. Linda and I had discussions about this. His ten-year-old son, Wade, had often been at our house, starved for attention, as was Wade's sister, Victoria, who was the same age as David. Ewing was uninterested in his own children and certainly wouldn't have any interest in mine. I thought, *Linda should know, that alone should have been enough to disqualify him as a replacement for me.* My children already had a father, a father who loved them more than anything in this world, a father who would always put them first. This man was *not going to become their full-time father,* I proclaimed angrily to myself. I was a far better father and it appeared I was a better parent than Linda herself. I had read as many bedtime stories, given as many baths, and changed as many diapers as she had. I had every right to remain active and full-time in their lives. This was her choice. She had decidedly, willfully, irresponsibly deferred her responsibilities for the children to me for weeks. I had an inkling of what lay ahead, but the direction in which this was going was not favorable to me or to the children.

 Her attitude made it clear she was deeply embroiled in this affair and that she had no intention of ending it. That meant for me to have a continuing dominant presence in the children's lives, a colossal effort on my part would be necessary to secure custody. I would have to give the acting performance of a lifetime for which I was ill prepared. A mountain of evidence against her would be necessary to dissuade the court from the usual outcome in awarding children to the mother, and all the while, I would need to pretend not to know the heartbreaking news that was now so clear. Their folly would be their brazen behavior, their overconfidence, their arrogance, their carelessness, and their underestimation of my commitment to my children.

 A monumental task lay before me, almost impossible to achieve! The wife I loved for more than thirteen years had become an adversary. I had always been in love with her, but never sure of her devotion to me, and now it appeared my uncertainty had been justified. I knew the coming battle would be bitterly contentious and, if I lost, Ewing likely would become my children's full-time parent with dreadful consequences for both the children and me. It was me against them, and the children were my life now. But they were at risk. The only advantage I had was that I was the only one who knew what was going on except for Linda and Ewing, I thought.

 I drove home quickly from Ewing's office, knowing that she would likely stop to pick up groceries to legitimize her ploy of "shopping" and that if I hurried, I could get home before she did. I turned onto our street with our 4,200-square-foot home in view. It was the home of our dreams, which we had planned and built together. We had just completed construction at about the time Jade was born in June 1976. Now, this beautiful home that we'd built together with years of careful thought and planning for our family would forever be changed—no longer a refuge of comfort, happiness, and love, but a temporary place where the outrageous events of the next few weeks would play out.

Linda arrived home with groceries from her afternoon tryst. The children and I were in the den as though we'd been at home the entire afternoon.

"Did Susan call?" she asked.

"There haven't been any calls," I said, sensing now that Linda's friend, Susan Johnson, was playing a supporting role in this caper, as well.

"She was going to call to tell you I would be running a little late."

"No, no call," I responded curtly.

I went into the bathroom and held my head over the bowl, hearing Linda's voice in my head. A few moments passed. Then I threw up. *Is this real? Is this really happening?* I stared at myself in the mirror, shaking my head in disbelief, trying to find out what it was about me that had become so objectionable to her.

As she began fixing dinner, she asked "Are we trimming the tree tonight?"

"That was the plan," I snapped back at her angrily, my acting performance conducted poorly.

At the dinner table, the only words spoken were in response to the children's chatter. Every cell of my body trembled, and I had a nearly uncontrollable urge to blurt out all I knew. But I could not put the children, these two little ones, at risk. I would have to hold myself together for an indeterminate time. Just me against Linda and that poor excuse of a doctor, neighbor, and friend who I had trusted and now wanted to kill with my bare hands; the man I had allowed to treat my wife medically. *What husband typically has any say in his wife's choice of her gynecologist?* I thought, *It's always the wife's choice. What husband ever weighs in on that decision? How much fault do I share in this?*

"How was shopping?" I asked, sarcastically.

"Fine."

"What all did you buy?" I responded, now offended, and disgusted at the charade that was going on between us.

"I didn't buy anything but groceries. You can go shopping and not buy anything, you know. That's what happened today," the favor of my sarcasm now returned to me.

Accepting her indignant reply, I gathered the children to take them upstairs to the tub, away from their mother who was now nauseating me. I let them play in their bath a little longer than usual while my thoughts echoed the details of her mistreatment of me for weeks and the presumed raunchy exploits of her bawdy afternoon rendezvous. Washing them fondly, I kept thinking, *it would be over my dead body that they would take these children from me.*

Did Linda have any idea what she was doing? Was she in her right mind? She had lit a fuse that was going to blow up in her face, I thought; continuing to soak in my love for the two innocent little ones in the bathtub who had become my focus, all the while, fearing the possibility that she could get the children, jettison me, and Ewing would become their full-time parent.

You build your whole life around your wife and children, and, seemingly in an instant, it's all taken away and you're reduced to a visiting parent forevermore, having little to no impact on their lives. Two self-centered people in heat were thinking only of themselves and nothing of the havoc they would wreak on the lives of their families.

I let the water dribble from the washcloth down their backs and the nape of their necks. Linda was in the kitchen rinsing off each plate and utensil before she put them in the dishwasher. I was doing the same with the children, drying them off and putting on their night clothes.

David remembered the Christmas tree we were to decorate that evening; and he was anxious to get started. I was feeling dread but would not deny him his enjoyment. Finished with their baths, we came downstairs, each child holding my hand, and we went directly to the den where the Christmas tree was. Linda ambled in and we began to decorate the tree, the kids excitedly picking out each colored ornament, the younger child taking longer than the elder. One at a time the children brought them over to either Linda or me, and together we put them on the tree carefully; almost in silence, at a time together that should have been joyful and fun. The children surely sensed the tension between us. I felt so bad for them for what was happening to them, keeping my anger inside at their mother for precipitating these circumstances; the consequences of which would impact their lives and ours forever. And it was Christmastime!

After a while, I left the room and went into the master bedroom bath to check whether the diaphragm had reappeared. The case was still empty. Outraged, but under control, because I knew I had to be, I returned to the living room to the Christmas tree and tried to make the best of the evening, for the children's sake.

I had tried so hard to be the husband she could love. I loved her so much prior to all of this. But now, she had made it impossible for me to act in a loving, caring, or gentle way. I was not a good actor, although that is exactly what I had to do, and I didn't do the best job of concealing my inner ire at her, as well as at myself. I had likely tried too hard with Linda over the years and was learning that when there is little to no love returned, one's efforts are likely to have the opposite effect. When you're overly effusive about your love, as I had been in my attempts to regain her affections at that time, you look even more preposterous, and the efforts are a complete turn-off.

The tree was done. I took the children upstairs and tucked them in. Their mother seemed content to defer these responsibilities to me these days. I assumed it was because she was thinking that shortly I'd be absent from the house and not available to sub for her, so, the only really nice thing she was doing for me these days was allowing me a lot of time with the children. I was to be a short timer in their lives. And, of course, my stepping in to care for the children provided her time to devote to her new extracurricular interests.

I could hear Linda getting ready for bed. For four nights she had slept alone, suggesting we wait until after the holidays to separate because it would be too upsetting for the children to do so during the Christmas season; as well David's fifth birthday was December 28th.

I was no longer good enough to be her husband. I was consumed by the thought; I couldn't make sense of it. It didn't matter how much I loved her. It didn't matter how hard I had tried or how good I had been to her. It didn't matter that I was the father of her children or that I was a good father. I couldn't be enough to satisfy her. I had no idea what had gone wrong or what I was guilty of, but I was no longer adequate. Someone else had more to offer her and had displaced me. I had been good enough to be her husband until a better opportunity came along, as though my allotted time with her had expired. Even before her "I don't love you anymore" announcement, I probably should have known something was wrong from her unspoken words, her actions, and her unwillingness to have any constructive dialogue with me. But I had been unsuspecting and probably hesitant to rock the proverbial boat without having more information about the circumstances. After our many years together without any such difficulty, I certainly didn't suspect what had become reality.

Now I knew what I should have known earlier without her having to tell me. Without any definitive plan in mind for her husband, she was in the midst of an exciting new relationship with her doctor - her gynecologist - who was offering her experiences she had never had before. Across the street was this man - our neighbor - who was enjoying my wife; and now, under the circumstances, going forward, for as long as it took, I would deliberately allow this to continue as a plan of action to be played out - the only prudent option I had, as painful as that was. This was devastating to me; but her resolve had been on full display. She was not coming back; and I had no intention of waiting for the axe to fall.

Upstairs in the room to which I had been relegated, I put my hands behind my head and stared up at the dark. Consumed by silence and loneliness, I didn't know how I was going to keep it all together. Conflicted and pulled in different directions, part of my brain was hoping she would have an epiphany and reverse herself, that we'd have the opportunity somehow to work things out, although I had no idea how I would ever be able to forgive and forget, if she would want to do that. *Would it be possible?* It would not. Things would get worse. I remained torn between what I knew I had to do and my thoughts of the possibility, however slim, that she would reverse herself to save our family - if only for the sake of our children. But something else was more important to her now, and she was absorbed in her new interest. I felt sick and in pain but didn't know whether it was pain over love lost, the loss of my family, or the loss of the idea of family. I was not sure which it was, and I was not sure for a very long time—years, as it would turn out.

During the night, I entered her bedroom and eased by my sleeping wife to the master bathroom to again check the diaphragm. It still hadn't been put back into its case. Then I spotted her purse. I picked it up and took it upstairs with me where I went through it, seeing her small 1979 calendar notebook containing two telephone numbers for "Jimmy"- his personal residence number and his private office telephone number. After several hours I returned to her room, looking down at her peaceful, sleeping face. Replacing the purse, I went into the bathroom again to check on the diaphragm. There it was, leaning on its side against the cold-water faucet. Since my last trip to the bathroom, she had woken up and removed it, rinsed it off and left it there to dry, like a round, rubber mini Ten Commandments. It looked proud of itself. It seemed to say "These aren't the Old Commandments. These are the New Commandments." Again, sickish, I made my way quietly past her out and to my room upstairs. Back in bed, I lay awake in torment for hours until finally, in the early morning hours, I fell into an exhausted sleep.

CHAPTER TWO

We were students at Jacksonville University in Florida in 1965 and 1966. I was a Junior and a residence hall monitor when Linda arrived to register for a dormitory as a freshman. My task that day was to check new students in. Spotting this beautiful young freshman in line to register, I nudged my counterpart aside to position myself to greet her. I remember thinking a thought I'd never had before: *Here is the girl I'm going to marry.* There was such an innocence about her. My heart was pounding. For an instant, I couldn't look at her. Then, suddenly, she was right before me. "Linda Dickerson" she announced, as our eyes met for the first time, and I acted as though I had it all together. There was a trace of a smile in those lovely eyes, as if she even knew something already. Upon meeting her, I found her to be as I had envisioned: approachable, pleasant, dignified, conversant, all-together; and I was definitely physically attracted to her.

Two months later, our first date took place on a beautiful starry night, just like the thousands of nights I hoped we would share. *Such a beautiful girl*, I kept thinking, already dreaming of marriage, ridiculous as that may have been. We were in the clouds metaphorically—at least I was—having dinner atop the highest building in Jacksonville in a revolving restaurant with a 360-degree panoramic view of the city, busting my college-student budget.

    Our conversation was casual and easy. There were two cherry tomatoes in my salad, and when I attempted to penetrate one with my fork, the rogue object took flight from the bowl to my lap, causing us both to erupt into awkward laughter. Inwardly, I was embarrassed at my awkwardness. *This could be the worst moment of my life*, I thought. I felt like an idiot. The tomato felt like it weighed a ton. I hoped she wasn't thinking she should be up here revolving with someone else. As a smile broke across her face, however, I joined in with a smile of my own and we seemed to be closer than we were supposed to be. I kept seeing Linda all that fall; by sheer persistence I seemed to have edged out other competitors. After a while, seeing each other became a thing that was assumed.

    I remember the first kiss - I had not wanted to be too forward and so waited for that right moment. It was our third date. It happened in the parking lot of her dorm near the end of an evening out. It had been an especially nice evening together and it ended deep in that kiss. The first time we made love was memorable - as much as it could be in a *1957* Chevrolet. We were parked in a lover's lane on a bluff, overlooking the harbor with the night out there in front of us. Barriers that had stopped us before instead lifted, and we went with our feelings in the closed darkness of that car. It happened. The sudden trembling of her body, the way she held tighter to me in all that night that surrounded us—it was like nothing I had ever felt before. I knew I loved her - her touch, her responses, the way she yielded to me. That feeling lingered between us in our silence as we drove back toward the dorm. While I'd had a few other short-lived relationships with Linda I knew this was what they wrote songs about. I knew it out on the beach where we went at times to relax on weekends, sometimes staying the afternoons into the evenings after dark. We'd bring food, drinks, and cook hot dogs on a fire, taking shelter in the hollows behind the dunes, out of the wind. There we could lay on a blanket in each other's arms, making love behind the dunes, enjoying the breaking of the surf close by.

In the spring of 1967, Linda left school to be with her parents in Chile, South America, where her father was with Allied Chemical in Santiago. Jacksonville University was on the trimester system, and I continued classes at JU throughout the summer, as I was double-majoring and planned to go to graduate school. Linda and I communicated by letters during the summer. My good friend Tommy Hanes, the incoming student government president, kept asking me, "Have you heard anything?" I sensed Tommy was envious of my relationship with Linda and was simply fishing for details. He had asked too many times for me not to be suspicious. I'd tell him as little as possible. I didn't think he needed to know. And so it went that summer.

When Linda returned to school in August to resume studies, she announced that she wanted to date others. To my surprise, despite his and my friendship, Tommy had made his move, having written to her throughout the summer without any hint of that to me. My love for Linda was unwavering, but hers for me was not. Obviously, it never was, and it never would be.

In the fall of '66, I continued calling and dating Linda, while she kept herself open and available for others. Eventually, however, the competition fell away including my good friend Tommy (our friendship was never the same again), and I began to feel more secure in the relationship with Linda.

In April of 1967, I graduated from Jacksonville University and entered East Carolina University in Greenville, North Carolina, to pursue graduate work in geology. Linda and I commuted the long distance several times that fall, visiting each other over long weekends. She now seemed to share the same degree of love for me that I had for her. I began to think, with the cost of traveling back and forth on weekends, we could live together in North Carolina a lot cheaper.

On one visit, I picked her up from Raleigh Airport. Sky high, driving from Raleigh to Greenville, I pulled the car over, told her I wanted to marry her, and asked her to marry me.

A smile burst from her face, and she threw her arms around me. "When?", she replied.

"As soon as possible," I said, ecstatic. "Now."

We married on December 23, 1967, in South River, New Jersey, before family and friends. I was as happy as I had ever been. I loved her then and thought it would last forever. We flew by helicopter from Newark Airport to Kennedy and spent our wedding night at a Holiday Inn at the airport, where we were to fly out the next morning to Bermuda for our honeymoon. A new element was added to our lives. We were husband and wife, officially responsible to each other.

Linda forgot to pack sensible shoes. She hobbled around for three days in her high heels and cursed herself for her stupidity, but we managed to ride motor bikes and even dance. We basked in the sun, enjoyed wonderful food, good music, and most of all, mutual love. We returned home to a new life with great hope, faith and trust that didn't need to be spoken.

I had a 6-year obligation with the US Navy and after completing graduate school, I was on active duty for three years. We then moved to Florence, South Carolina where I taught geology and geography at Francis Marion College for a couple of years before going into the real estate business. Real Estate was far more lucrative than teaching school with only a master's degree, even at the college level.

David was born six years into our marriage. Jade, born two years later, was delivered by Dr. James Ewing. Life was good and there was great promise that summer of 1978. The success of my business provided the income needed for a comfortable lifestyle. Within two years of David's birth, we had built our dream home, moving in just before Jade was born in June 1976. We had two precious children and a new home large enough to accommodate even more children. We were members of the local country club, where we enjoyed dining, dancing, and other social events. I played tennis there at the club. We spent a lot of time working together in our yard, planting shrubs and flowers, raking leaves, tidying up the driveway and walkways that adorned our property. We settled into a pleasant familiar routine. Our lives had moved in the direction of our dreams. Our hopes were becoming reality, and I felt Linda was as content as I was. Each evening as I turned into our street from work and I caught a glimpse of our home, I experienced a deep sense of pride and satisfaction knowing how comfortable my wife and children were. I knew I had been blessed and I was grateful. Those were the best of times for me. Everything had been cued up for an idyllic life ahead, as found in an especially good novel.

But, in the fall of 1978 things inexplicably took a turn for the worse. Dr. Ewing and his family had moved into our neighborhood, three doors down and across the street. He and his wife would occasionally stop by our home in the evenings for an after-dinner walk around the neighborhood. Linda joined them. I stayed home with the children to start their evening routine prior to bedtime. Months later in court, I would hear how they had invited me on these walks with them, but I "would not go." This was to claim that I was anti-social; when, of course, one of us had to stay home with the children. Reflecting, I recalled times when his wife was not at our back door with him when he picked up Linda. I assumed she was waiting at the end of our driveway at the street for them to join her, as I had seen on earlier occasions. Wrong! How stupid was that of me! I should have known. I missed a lot of signs; that one in particular. At some point—the precise moment would always be a puzzle to me—Linda and her doctor's relationship became much more than just patient and friend.

It wasn't as though she had announced one day, "Vernon, I don't love you anymore. I filed papers today for divorce." Rather, she had slithered off, cat-like, to her surreptitious illicit encounters, leaving those who loved her behind, unenlightened, trusting her, but betrayed.

CHAPTER THREE

When it dawned on me what was going on as I was swinging the children in the backyard that first Wednesday in December, I knew instantly, instinctively, that I had lost my wife, and that it would be my word against hers (theirs). To better my chances of success, I needed to know the details of what was going on, and in order to get those details, I had to hear what they were saying to each other. As important, if not more so, would be my ability to produce proof. And this would necessitate recordings of their telephone conversations. I would have to tap our telephone.

The next day, Thursday morning, December 7th, I went to Dixie Radio, an electronics supply store in Florence where I secured a spare telephone and items necessary to complete a wiretap. So it wouldn't be suspected I was doing something illegal, I told the clerk I needed a device that would allow me to record business telephone conversations. I wasn't sure the store would be able to sell me such a device. It was not clear to me what the ramifications of wiretapping were at that time, but it didn't really matter, as I was determined to do what I had to do regardless. I knew that without incontrovertible evidence, my testimony alone would not be enough. This was a doctor I was up against. I was just an average Joe. This was the direction in which events were headed. I had no idea how instrumental the wiretap would be, nor the issues it would cause me.

That night, after I was sure Linda was asleep, in the corner of the closet of the bedroom I was in, I connected the extension phone. I extended the telephone wire I had bought earlier that day from the bedroom to the junction box at the back corner of the house. To do this, I entered the attic, the entrance of which was on the same floor as the upstairs bedrooms. Above the bedrooms, with telephone wire, flashlight, and screwdriver in hand, I approached the gable end of the house, punching a small hole through the screen vent through which I dropped the end of the telephone wire to the ground below. All the while, I was thinking what a devious, and, perhaps, despicable thing it was to do, even to an unfaithful wife. But the children were foremost in mind at this point, and I'd have done anything I had to do to protect them.

I dropped enough wire to the ground to reach the junction box at the rear corner of the house, and then extended the remaining wire across the top of the bedrooms and down the attic wall to the rear of the closet of my bedroom. I ran the wire underneath the insulation on the backside of the closet wall so it would not be readily seen, and then punched a hole through the sheetrock stud wall into the closet—the closet that would become a torture chamber for me in the coming days and weeks. In the closet, I cut off the end of the wire and attached the wire to the spare phone. I disconnected the ringer to silence it. Quietly, I crept downstairs and out of the house into the night to connect the other end of the wire on the ground to the terminal posts in the junction box - red to red, green to green.

I was concerned about the exposed wire coming from the vent in the gable end of the house stretching diagonally across the house's brick façade to the junction box. It could now be seen, even in the dark of night with the moonlight, but I was hoping Linda would be too preoccupied with her adulterous entanglement to notice in the daytime. Also, I had a very bright, inquisitive, and observant son I already expected would become an engineer someday who might notice this strange new wire extending from the ridge of the house and say something about it to his mother. That was a concern. With the connection complete, I had only to connect the small black box, the tapping device. It was a simple connection to the box and then a plug from the black box to a cassette tape recorder. I prayed the wiretap was operational. *All this effort necessary*, I thought, *instead of working through issues, instead of taking care of and enjoying our children together, caring for our home and enjoying the fruits of all we had accomplished in our eleven-year marriage, thirteen-year relationship.* Linda's choice of dalliance over loyalty and impulse over commitment was the height of irresponsibility.

I lay on my bed, unable to sleep; eventually, conscious of daybreak, I awoke exhausted to another day of the same nightmarish situation. I made breakfast for the children. Linda was sleeping in, I presumed, in total comfort, absorbed with the affair she was enjoying. I never understood how she could be so preoccupied to the exclusion of and without conscience for deeds so destructive to her family.

The next day was Friday, December 8th. All day at work, I kept thinking about the wiretap. I kept thinking about that sleazy Ewing who had maneuvered his way into my life, manipulating his way into the heart and mind of my wife. I knew that in some countries it was permissible to simply blow away a guy named Mohammad or Farooq. You blew him away and walked right out of the courtroom to a cheering crowd, with guys slapping you on the back except the relatives of Mohammad or Farooq. But in this country that might not be the case. And besides, the children were my priority, and it was not likely a family court would award children to someone who had just killed someone else, regardless of the reason.

What would I find that evening when I got to my room where the eavesdropping device was hidden in the corner of the closet? Had my secret been discovered by my wife, or my inquisitive son? How deeply involved in this affair had she become? How serious was she? What was being said about me? What were their plans? What was Linda's mindset about all of this? I knew the evidence I had to this point could be considered only circumstantial evidence - that much more would be needed.

Sickening as it was to dwell on what was occurring with Linda and Ewing, I shifted my thinking to the children. From the pressure of it all, I felt I was going to burst. Fly apart. That evening, after an awkwardly quiet dinner and taking care of the children, I left Linda in front of the TV and went up to my room and locked the door. I waited. And waited.

After at least an hour had passed, I quietly eased out of my room to the landing at the top of the stairway. I could hear her talking softly on the phone downstairs. I could tell—there was no doubt in my mind - she was talking to him. I prayed the wiretap was working, then went back to my room, locking the door behind me. I removed the luggage and blankets I had placed on top of the black box and tape recorder to conceal them in the closet, and I saw the tape recorder advancing. The extension telephone and wiretap were working! She was talking to him. I waited for the recorder to stop advancing, which signaled an end to their conversation, and for Linda to go to her bedroom for the evening. I played back the tape from the day's recordings; hearing for the first time the voices targeted by my wiretap:

Ewing: "Hello."
Linda: "Hi."

The mere sound of their greeting each other sent a chill through me.

Ewing: "Where's Doohickey?"

I now had an alias.

Linda: "He's upstairs in his room, probably asleep. He has been going up there after supper and after the children are put to bed."
Ewing: "Have you decided when you're going to move him out?"

At that moment, I couldn't have been more stunned or offended. *So, it is me that is the offending party and needs to go? This is outrageous!*

Linda: "No, not yet."
Ewing: "Well, it sure will be better when you get him out of the house so I can *get* to you easier. If he were not so close, I'd come over and check you out tonight. Would you like that?"

Right away, it was obvious this man had a myopic focus on sex. He had a one-track mind! I thought, *I guess when you're a hammer, all you see are nails.*

Linda: "Yes, that would be nice."

    Hearing this vivid confirmation of my suspicions of Linda in her very own voice was like a sucker punch to the gut and a bowling ball thrown at my heart.

Ewing: "You're not flowing yet, are you?"
Linda: "No, not for another week yet."
Ewing: "Guess I'll have to get my licks in this week then. Have you been preparing yourself for me?"
Linda: "Yes, but it's hard for me still, even though you've told me what to do."

    What was this? I was feeling more inadequate than ever, emasculated. Was he speaking of something she could do herself to prepare for more sexual excitement for him? I didn't know precisely what he was referring to. I hadn't gone to school to become a gynecologist.

Ewing: "Really wish I could come fuck you right now."

    This didn't sound to me like the kind of conversation a revered physician should be having with a patient. Nor did it sound like conversation Linda would condone. Why was she allowing him to talk to her in this disrespectful manner? It was beyond me. I had a lot to learn! Had she become so debased? She obviously was subjecting herself to the whims of this repulsive deviate, compliant to his urges. He had her right where he wanted her. This was both heartbreaking and maddening.

Linda: "Yes."

This is not happening, I thought, sick at heart and beginning to get sick to my stomach. Who had my wife become? Had she been like this all along and I never stirred this part of her being? There was something this guy was triggering inside her, something I had never touched, and I was beginning to get a little sense of what it was.

Ewing: "I could get you off like you've never known. You don't think he'd mind, do you? He could join us… Oh, that would be interesting…No, I don't want him around. I want you for myself. I'm going to get you, you know."

The crassness of this statement pushed me to full-blown nausea. How does anyone get like this?

Linda: "Yes, I believe you will, Jimmy."

Hearing her tawdry reply made my heart sink to its lowest level ever. She found him attractive!

Linda: "Oh… I forgot, sorry, meant to tell you I had to hang up quickly yesterday. He was right at the back door."
Ewing: "We'll just have to exercise patience. But in the meantime, save it for me. You know I care for you. Save that fuck for me. It will be so much better when he's not around."

Could she not see that "I care for you" was as hollow as a toilet paper tube? Could she not see the emptiness of his next words revealing his out-of-control, runaway train quest for sexual gratification? Had she gone morally blind to this kind of behavior?

It was just so painfully hard to understand how a man who would talk to her this way would be attractive to her, even if he had other redeeming qualities. She should have been repulsed by such a person. Instead, she was compliant. What was the appeal? And his lack of self-dignity seemed to inspire her own commensurate drop in self-worth. Scattered thoughts filled my mind. Had she wanted disrespect from me like this? Maybe she wouldn't be discussing tossing me out like an old, nasty dish rag, if I had treated her in the demeaning way Ewing was treating her. But could I have? I'd had too much respect for her, for almost any woman. Being gentle and being a gentleman with her had gotten me this! *How's that working for you, Vernon? Not!* Yet I couldn't stop thinking, *How in the world did Linda get to this level of moral decay so quickly?*

My thoughts swirled. *The audacity of this filthy degenerate calling himself a doctor! My God! My innocent little children! This reprobate was going to replace me in their lives*; and my wife was conspiring with him! *Over my dead body! Not so long as there is breath in me!*

Stunned and appalled by the vulgar content of this first recording, physically exhausted and emotionally drained, I slumped over on the floor of my closet. When I awoke and looked at my watch, it was 4:30 a.m. I was again feeling sick to my stomach. I went into the bathroom to see if I could throw up, but I could not. Whatever had been in my stomach had already been expelled earlier in the evening.

On that night that was dark in so many ways, so many years ago, I had no choice but to acknowledge the attraction Linda had to her doctor, with whom I could not compete. So, what was this difference she found in him, other than his being a doctor? Among other differences, the one that stood out most in my mind was what certain women desperately want, including Linda (something I could not be): a "Bad Boy," a man who is bold, domineering, demanding, unpredictable, arrogant, uber masculine, sexy, determined to get what he wants, selfish, deceitful. I could hear in my head the Fleetwood Mac song, "Players only love you when they're playin'."

"Bad Boys" are also full of it! And Ewing was no different. He fit the description to a T. I was sure that when young Jimmy was growing up, at Christmastime, given the choice to tell Santa how he'd been for the year, he would claim proudly to have been naughty over nice every time and not care one-bit what Santa or anyone else thought. I knew some women can't get enough of this kind of man. The emotional excitement and psychological attraction are all-consuming, and no amount of reasoning can sway them otherwise. They're off in a new lane and there's no return, especially once sex becomes a fact.

In sharp contrast to the "Bad Boy," Linda's life with me, in her eyes, had evidently become the opposite—I was too predictable, compliant, passive, servicing, humdrum, boring. Both Ewing's aggressive personality and his doctor title fed her drive. It was a dance! Enamored she was!

Another explanation occurred to me: perhaps her dalliance was a result of boredom with life as a mother stuck at home all day with children. She had complained to me about this very thing—that I was out in the stimulating business world, interacting with grown people all day, every day, while she was stuck at home with two kids and chores. Or perhaps it was a bout of delayed postpartum depression. Or—and here my musings really began to solidify—maybe it was the inevitable result of all the elements together: the scientific fact that the peak of sex drive in a woman is age thirty and - with the means to explore its fulfillment - adding this to her fascination with her doctor, the dynamics of the "Bad-Boy" attraction, and boredom of life as a stay-at-home mother, the ingredients existed for a perfect storm for an affair. That had to be it! Her salacious actions were the inevitable result of all these elements. It all added up!

Of course, the boundary to such irresponsible actions for any one of us is our conscience, that inner sense of right and wrong. How well we listen to and act upon our conscience is directly proportional to the authenticity and quality of our human relationships since it determines if and how our deeper emotional, intellectual, spiritual needs get met. Or, if it's only physical needs that are met, how those other needs don't get met. For example, looking back now with the ability to see it all clearly, I know the deep fulfillment I experienced while playing with, caring for, and loving our children was not something Linda experienced. Her eyes were focused elsewhere for some very powerful, instinctive reasons. In pursuit of her "fix" made possible with the exotic, erotic "Bad Boy" as catalyst and guide, Linda had completely abandoned her conscience.

Obviously, even though she could see that the price of abandoning her conscience might be very high, she still was willing to take that risk. She had a choice. We all do. Our choices and the thoughts that precede them are where we do or don't listen to and act upon what our conscience tells us. Assuredly, there are certain thoughts and choices of a viler nature that tend to make us blind to the consequences of the actions they inspire. I suppose that explains why Linda could not, or maybe she would not, see those consequences. Either way, we all wind up living with the consequences of our thoughts and actions. And, beyond life, the greatest consequence of one's actions impacts our legacy and how we are remembered. As Maximus Decimus Meridius said in the movie *Gladiator*, "What we do in life… echoes in eternity."

CHAPTER FOUR

The next day, the shocking reality of the wiretap's content yielded clarity of what actions I needed to take next. As much as it made me ill to think of what Ewing was doing with my wife, I had to allow the affair to continue for as long as it might take to gain whatever advantage I could in the interim. I had no idea how long this would be and whether I could contain everything within myself until there was enough evidence to support my claims.

A private detective would be needed to validate my wife's illicit activities. And I needed an attorney - the best attorney possible. The mayor of Florence, who was a close friend, contacted the city police chief for the recommendation of a local detective. The chief referred Charles Ray who I called immediately and then met with him in his home that day. It was Saturday afternoon, December 9th. Charles agreed to begin surveillance immediately. He understood the importance of the outcome to me and quickly recommended Jan Warner from Sumter, South Carolina as the best domestic litigant attorney in the state. Charles gave me Jan's direct phone number. I was confident Jan was the right choice for me when my personal attorney recommended Jan as well without having to give it any thought at all. He warned me, however, that I should "be prepared for extraordinary expenses; maybe even going broke," he joked. (little did he know!)

The children and I spent the afternoon at the Methodist Park, a couple blocks from the house. There were large concrete pipes they could crawl through, a jungle gym, a slide, and a seesaw. I couldn't help but reflect back on happier times when the children and Linda and I had spent time at this park before she'd begun having sex with her gynecologist. After I returned home with the children, she arrived at 5:30 carrying a small package - her iron-clad proof that she had been shopping. Charles Ray's first report was delivered the next morning:

> 1:00 p.m. - Agent set up surveillance on the Baumrind residence.
>
> 1:55 p.m. - Mrs. Baumrind departed her residence in her automobile where she went directly to the Medical Center Building in front of the Memorial Hospital. She exited her vehicle and entered Dr. Ewing's office. The doors were locked after Mrs. Baumrind's entrance. Agent continued surveillance of Dr. Ewing's office.
>
> 4:50 p.m. - Mrs. Baumrind departed Dr. Ewing's. Agent discontinued surveillance at this time.

This report served to layer on more pain and sadness.

Like all nights now, I didn't sleep well. In the morning, I made breakfast for the children and not wanting to have to have any conversation with Linda under the circumstances, I left for my office. It was December 10th. Today was the day of a children's Christmas party at the country club. I returned home at lunchtime. Jade was put down for her nap time and David and I left the house to attend the party at the club. While David was entertained and preoccupied with the party, I called Jan Warner. Extraordinarily gifted, Jan would become the most important person in my life in the next several years, not including my children. He and I spoke briefly about the circumstances, and he gave me a 10:00 appointment for the next morning. In my absence from home that day, the recording device picked up the following conversation between Linda and her best friend, Susan.

Linda: "Hello."
Susan: "Hi, *how* are things going?"
Linda: "All right."
Susan: "So tell me what happened yesterday afternoon? You just went down there and had a nice visit?"
Linda: "Yes. A nice time,"
Susan: "Ohhhh! *A* nice time!"
Linda: "Yes, nice visit. Whatever you want to say."
Susan: (clearly eager to hear more) "More than talk?"
Linda: "Oh, I don't know."
Susan: "What do you mean you don't know?"
Linda: "Well, I think it's kind of private."
Susan: "Oh, now it's private. Last week it wasn't."
Linda: "Well, you can guess. Okay?"
Susan: "No. I'm not going to guess."
Linda: "Okay. I'11 see you Tuesday afternoon then."
Susan: "Right! I'll stop by."
Linda: "Okay, Bye."
Susan: "Bye,"

James Ewing was the gynecologist for both women. One of them had originally recommended Dr. Ewing to the other. Obviously, Linda had revealed the ongoing relationship to Susan and Susan was covering for her friend, providing support, including babysitting for Linda, and serving as an alibi by telling me they were "shopping" together when they weren't.

Susan called me that afternoon, feigning concern. "How are you getting along?" she asked. Of course, her real purpose for contacting me was to find out what I knew of what was going on. And, of course, I knew she didn't care at all how I was. Having heard their conversation earlier and knowing her duplicity, I told her only what I knew she was already aware of - that Linda and I had our differences, that we were not getting along and that I was worried and concerned about the situation. Susan knew I loved my wife. She assured me she would talk to Linda and try to help with improving matters between us. Susan had known us for more than a decade, which made her complicity doubly hard to take. *You know*, I thought, *a real friend tells you what you need to hear; not what you want to hear. Susan should be helping Linda make the right decisions, rather than aiding and abetting in the coverup for the juicy details.* That was the last call I ever took of hers.

On Monday, December 11th, I drove to Sumter to meet with Jan Warner. Upon greeting the receptionist, she handed me a very lengthy questionnaire to answer. In addition to a lot of basic required information including reasons for divorce to be provided were several pages and suggested "prime objectives client wishes to accomplish." I read through these objectives, skipping over all but "custody," which I circled, and at the end, I provided the children's personal information.

Jan was very cordial. He radiated competence and confidence. He looked over my responses in the questionnaire, noting my sole interest in only custody of the children, looked up beyond his desk at me and said, in his deep, resonant voice, "Obtaining custody anywhere in the US is very difficult for the father. In this state, it is almost unheard of, unless the mother is alcoholic, abusive, or is a hardened criminal. Is she any of these?"

I responded, "She's not an alcoholic and she's not a criminal. There are times I expect there is some abuse to our son, who's almost five." He noted my response and gave me the names and contact numbers for three child psychiatrists. He advised me to select one and see that doctor with the children.

I told Jan I had installed a wiretap on an extension phone that I had concealed in my bedroom, and he explained to me the possible repercussions of the wiretap. What I had done, he said, "…could be a direct violation of federal laws prohibiting such intrusion on the private conversations of another party." He suggested that I write him a check which he would forward to the Legal Research Group, Inc., along with his letter stating the specific facts of how the wiretap had been installed and requesting "an opinion on the legality of my actions." He explained that the Legal Research Group investigates specific legal issues, discovers precedents, and recommends appropriate procedures. Not having all the answers to legalities of the wiretap, Jan emphasized that I should say nothing to anyone about the case or the wiretap. In the meantime, he left to my discretion and peril whether I continued the tap which could have been illegal.

He then suggested that I coordinate what I was learning from the tap with the private detective and him, and emphasized the importance of my remaining silent and going along with the affair until he advised that we had adequate evidence to support our legal objectives. After hearing everything I had accomplished to date, his parting comment was, " If you follow my instructions explicitly, by the time your wife and the doctor learn what we know, we'll be so far ahead of them, they'll never catch us….Let's hope we can secure everything necessary to give ourselves the strongest case possible in the meantime. Let's hope she'll be as irresponsible and as careless as she is apparently capable of being."

"Never catch us" were the words that stood out for me and reverberated in my mind. Those words were the most encouraging I had heard from the beginning of all this. They were inspirational and would give me the strength to pull myself together in moments to come when I felt most discouraged.

CHAPTER FIVE

On Tuesday, December 12th, Linda had dinner ready when I got home. It was so hard to enter the house and act as though I didn't know what was going on when I was inwardly fuming. It simply wasn't possible to completely control the emotions inside me, and I was unable to act lovingly, torn by the truth and by my secret objective that demanded silence. My bad attitude incensed and emboldened her; making matters worse than they already were. I wondered how many other husbands in this world had to endure this kind of agony.

After dinner I played with David and Jade, then bathed them and tucked them in. My routine was typical now. I laid down with David and talked to him until, weary, I fell asleep. Waking about forty-five minutes later, the child was asleep, and I returned to my room, then, showered, and went to bed. I could not listen to the day's taped conversations because I couldn't do both that and leave the wiretap available to capture any conversation that might occur yet that evening.

In the early morning hours of the night, I listened to the day's recordings. The sound of Linda's sweet voice, that special, loving tone of hers which had once been reserved for me, but now was for someone else, tore at my soul. A morning conversation from the previous day had occurred.

DECEIT

Linda: "Hello."
Ewing: "Hello."
Linda: "Hi. How are you?"
Ewing: "Okay, what are you up to?"
Linda: "Oh, usual Monday duties - laundry."
Ewing: "I called you and must have missed you."
Linda: "You missed me? What time did you call?"
Ewing: "I called three or four times."
Linda: "You did? Oh, the phone rang once that I'm aware of, sometime around 9:30, but Louise [Ewing's wife] was here, and I didn't want to answer the phone in her presence, in case it was you."
Ewing: "But I didn't leave a message. That wasn't me."
Linda: "Oh."
Ewing: "The other calls must have been your other fellow."
Linda: "I'm sorry I missed you. I had some errands. I had to go to the bank and the grocery store and the post office."
Ewing: "Did you ever get Susan?"
Linda: "Yes."
Ewing: "Did Vernon call her?"
Linda: "Yes, he did."
Linda: "Five minutes before I called her."
Ewing: "Really?"
Linda: "Yes. So, he knows I lied. He hasn't confronted me with it yet. But he was real upset Saturday night and today. This morning he acted almost normal."

    I would have to ask God to help me through this. I could hear the wheels of Ewing's warped mind turning.

Ewing: "What did you tell him? That you went to Susan's or what?"

Linda: "He was questioning me somewhat and I wasn't giving him very much information. He wanted to know where I was. I named a few places, and I said I met up with Susan and I let it go at that. And then he asked if I had gone over to Susan's house? And so I said yes. When I was at your office Saturday, I thought about calling her right from there and then thought no, I won't do that. I'll wait until I get home and then, I forgot about it."

Ewing: "When did he call her?"

Linda: "Sunday afternoon when he took David to the Christmas show. He called her from the country club."

Ewing: "What did he ask her?"

Linda: "He asked her if she saw me and she said, 'I haven't seen Linda since Thursday.' So he said, 'I don't know what she's up to.' Susan said, 'Well, aren't things getting any better?' And he said, 'No, they're worse. She won't discuss our problems with me. She won't go to counseling. She's walking away from me.' That's what he said. I don't know. I really don't feel that bad about him knowing. He'll know sooner or later, so what's the difference? Has he gotten in touch with you yet?"

Ewing: "No."

Linda: "…I'm just going to tell him about you. Do you have any suggestions? I don't think I ought to try and tell him another lie."

Ewing: "Well, if he asks you why you lied to him, tell him the counselor told you to. Right?"

DECEIT

Linda: "Well, I guess so, but he didn't tell me to lie. He just said Vernon should never know about you if we were trying to patch things up."
Ewing: "I don't know how he's going to react"
Linda: "I could be mean and say, ha-ha-ha or something like that. That would be mean though. I don't know, he'll probably say, 'Well, I suspected it all along.' I was trying to keep out of his way. I was fixing supper the other night and he came over and said, 'I don't know what you're thinking, but I hope you make the right decision.'"

The two of them said nothing about the impact all of this would have on anyone but themselves. They were two self-centered people considering only what they wanted for themselves at that moment.

Ewing: Louise and I could see your Christmas tree lights through your window from the street. One night, if Vernon is not there, you could call Louise, and if he's there, you could mention that we had wanted to see the tree, if it was okay with him."
Linda: "Okay."
Ewing: "See what he says."
Linda: "Okay."
Ewing: "If he makes a big deal of it, forget it."
Linda: "You know the lady next door? Rhoda. Her father died yesterday. He was about seventy-eight. I had to bake a cake quickly for them. They're real nice people."
Ewing: "You know them pretty well?"
Linda: "Our driveways are side by side."
Ewing: "Does she know your situation?"

Linda: "No! Oh, no. They think we're the perfect couple. Like everybody else thinks. We've always been the perfect couple…everywhere we've been. The prince and the princess! That's what her daughter said about us. Little do they know."

Ewing: "Well, after I started seeing you, you told me it wasn't all that bad. Just sounded like you didn't want to get rid of him."

Linda: "He has many good points. He's very understanding. He loves the children, and he tries so hard to be such a good father. He's been good to me. He'll have a right to be angry with me."

Ewing: "You have such a good reputation. Maybe you ought to take this like it is. You've got the perfect Vernon."

Linda: "I don't think I love him as I once did, since you and I met."

Ewing: "You know, I helped draw - I tried to draw y'all apart, but you know deep down I feel like I'm responsible."

    I knew this man had no conscience. He was just playing the role; *a player just toying with his victim,* I thought.

Linda: "Yeah. I can understand that."

Ewing: "You keep saying he has good points. You enjoy being with me?"

Linda: "Yeah, I do. You're a lot different than he is… well not a lot, but…"

Ewing: "I really wish you could be more liberal."

Linda: "I'm conservative. That's just not me."

Ewing: "Would you like to be different?"

Linda: "Well, not really, for my own satisfaction, but maybe for you. I seem to like the old, you know, conventional way, and you like to do, you know, more."

Ewing: "What do I like to do that you don't like?"
Linda: "Well, it's not that I don't like to do it, it's just that I don't need to do it…You seem to like to try all kinds of different positions, whereas I'm content with just one."
Ewing: "Which one?"
Linda: "Or two maybe." [laughs]
Ewing: "Thought you liked variety?"
Linda: "Well, I like to be, you know, close to you, you know, face to face, whereas some of those positions, you can't."
Ewing: "Never complained in any of them."
Linda: "Oh, I'm not complaining. I was just trying to answer your question."
Ewing: "Got to somehow teach you how to swallow."
Linda: "I don't think I can ever do that successfully."
Ewing: "Didn't like the taste too good?"
Linda: "It's not the taste. It's… I don't know."
Ewing: "The idea?"
Linda: "Maybe. Well, I guess so, if it's not the taste, it must be the idea."
Ewing: "Dirty?"
Linda: "No, not dirty [laughs] I don't know."
Ewing: "I like the taste of your tiddie….You're too conservative."
Linda: "Yeah, I guess I am. Do you feel like I'm too inhibited for you?"
Ewing: "Yes"
Linda: "Like swallowing it…just asking if that was one of the areas? What are some of the other areas?"
Ewing: [...tape was inaudible…]

✓ Linda: "Oh, God, no. No, I could never do that. No, I don't think so. Well, I'll try harder for you."
Ewing: […tape was inaudible…]
Linda: "Well, if I can learn to do them, I'll do them."
Ewing: […tape was inaudible…]
Linda: "No. No, don't talk like that."
Ewing: […tape was inaudible…]
Linda: "Well, I think it's whatever is comfortable for the two people involved. I don't think there's ever one right way…you start talking about all of this stuff and it just leads me to think that you wish I were a little more like the girls in the movies you've been showing me."
Ewing: […tape was inaudible…]
Linda: "Yeah, that's right and that's why I don't think I can be any different, and that worries me."
Ewing: […tape was inaudible…]
Linda: "No, but you still show me the movies and…well, I think one big difference between those girls and me is that, ah, they're just out for the joy of sex. I'm not just out for that."
Ewing: "But still, there's a joy."
Linda: "No, no, but I mean, I want to be, but I want to be tender with you, and you can't be tender when your partner is pouncing all over you."
Ewing: "I'm not bored with you yet."
Linda: "Well, it hasn't been that long and you're still trying to teach me. You might just give up on me one of these days."
Ewing: "You think he's going to ask you again if you're seeing someone?"

Linda: "I don't know if he is or not. I don't know...You're not afraid of him, are you?"
Ewing: "I don't guess it matters if I am or not. You think he'll shoot me in a moment of rage?"
Linda: "He'll probably kill me." [she laughs]
Ewing: "Does he get violent?"
Linda: "Vernon? No."
Ewing: "Couldn't you soften the blow?"
Linda: "I'll tell him the truth. That's what I'll to do… *as* the reason for the separation… No sense lying anymore."
Ewing: "Does he know you've made up your mind?"
Linda: "I don't think so. I haven't laid that on him yet. He knows I won't do anything before the holidays are over… Oh, wait a moment. I have to help the children with their coats. Let me call you back in a minute. Bye."
Ewing: "Okay, bye."

In my bedroom closet, I sat there in the dark, aware of the deepest part of my soul. Reflecting, I could hear her say that same simple word—"bye"- so lovingly to me in the past, in a time when there was sincerity and emotion behind her responses to me. There was a break in the conversation and then a resumption.

Ewing: "Hello. *That w*as a long minute."
Linda: "I had some other things I had to get done. And now I'm cooking."
Ewing: "What are you cooking?"
Linda: ''Well, it's called Hungarian Goulash, but it has a fancier name. Being a southerner, you'd know it as beef stroganoff. It's like beef in cubes, with gravy and you serve it over noodles - you wouldn't like that."

Ewing: "I don't like noodles much."
Linda: "You're a rebel, that's why. See, if you were a Yankee, you would be a noodle person. If you had European ancestors, you'd be a noodle person."
Ewing: "Wish we could spend some more time together."
Linda: "Yes."
Ewing: "You know, we've pretty much proven our compatibility."

Ever the conductor constantly directing their conversation back to the topic he preferred with her - ever the willing, compliant accomplice.

Linda: "I know."
Ewing: "There are a lot of things you've got to work on. Gotta get you into the advanced art of making love in a variety of ways."
Linda: "Well, you know, it's different when you've been together a long time and you have a routine with just one person with whom you take walks, ride bikes, watch TV with or complain about the kids and try to make ends meet."
Ewing: "Right. You've got expensive tastes. I don't know if I can afford you."
Linda: "But that wasn't me all my life. That's just recently."
Ewing: "Just since you've gotten used to it."
Linda: "Vernon buys me a lot".
Ewing: "I might not treat you as good as he does. Look around you."
Linda: "I guess so. You wouldn't be mean to me, would you?"
Ewing: "No, it's just that I'm not the type of person who showers you with gifts all the time, with surprises like that car and stuff."

DECEIT

Linda: "That's not necessary. If I were looking for material things, I would be happy right here. You're considerate. You've done little things for me that you didn't have to do."

Ewing: "Like what?"

Linda: "Remember the pretzels you gave me. And you fixed my key chain. You didn't have to do that. And you fixed the windshield wiper on my car."

Ewing: "You are always eating out. I'm not crazy about eating out."

Linda: "I'm not crazy about eating out a lot either. Once in a while. But we've been eating out a lot lately though. He's been trying hard to accommodate me right now, with it being Christmas and all. We've attended Christmas parties and events. But other than that, we don't go out that much".

Ewing: "Did he used to not spend much time with the kids?"

Linda: "Let's see. When he went into business on his own, he was at the office a lot and didn't have much time with David. When Jade came along that improved some. But now he spends a lot of time with them. I guess he knows the end is near. He's commented that it's going to kill him not to be able to see them every morning and every evening."

I turned off the tape. I could not continue to listen to this. Her calloused remarks, her speaking with casual disdain for the years of love, the many gifts—large and small - given as expressions of my love, always putting her first, always thinking of ways that would bring her pleasure—to her they had all been material things only. She didn't understand the loving impulse or unselfish gesture that had prompted them and was now attributing an equal measure of consideration to him for the gift of the pretzels, for fixing her key chain. My hopes of her mellowing were dashed. She was enraptured with him and had fallen in lust with him, I presumed, because I never heard her tell him she loved him. And, I never heard him say anything similar. After all, why would a spider be nice to a fly trapped in its web?

It was Wednesday, December 13th, a long week after my dawning in the backyard, and in spite of all that was taking place, Linda and I attended a country club Christmas party that night. I continued to try with her, hoping for a change of heart, while concealing what I knew. I couldn't help myself—I felt compelled to try and redirect her back to me. During the evening, I did everything in my power to make her feel loved, but every response from her was perfunctory and listless. Nothing I did was going to work!

The next night Linda came into the bathroom while I was bathing the children and said, "The Ewings noticed our Christmas tree through the window last night. Would you mind if I invite them over to see it?" I told her, through my teeth, that would be fine. I wasn't sure how sincere I sounded. As I got the children bedded down for the night, I thought about the agony of having to sit in my living room with Jim Ewing. But the children were in the balance. I'd do anything! This charade would have to continue. The pressure, anger and sadness were gradually escalating like a horrific version of Ravel's *Bolero*.

When the Ewings arrived, Linda met them at the door and invited them into the living room where the tree stood. I came into the living room from Jade's room. There was that smile of his; always that smile - that incessant, impish, insidious smile of his.

Ewing extended his hand. "Hi. Vernon." He grinned. "How are you tonight?" Never in my life had I had to exercise so much self-restraint. Never before and never again. I don't know how cordial or unfriendly I was, but I managed somehow to respond that I was well and thanked him. If I came across as an ogre of a husband, I didn't care. I looked across the room at Louise, studying her expressions and wondering how much she knew or suspected of the duplicity going on here between her good friend, Linda, and her husband. The irony of the situation struck me, and not for the first time - she and I each playing our respective roles in this performance, and if she indeed knew, each of us miserable unto ourselves.

I asked if I could fix them drinks. He asked for a coke and Louise and Linda had sprites. I didn't drink anything. I was feeling nauseated again.

"That is a Christmas tree," said Ewing, sipping his coke.

"It's just gorgeous. I love all those handmade ornaments," Louise said.

"We like it," Linda said. "We've had a real problem with falling needles."

I excused myself to check on the children and didn't return. I just couldn't. In my mind, I kept repeating to myself Jan Warner's exhortations: "…*We'll get so far ahead of them, they'll never catch us.*" This inspired me like ten virtual shots of adrenaline.

CHAPTER SIX

I came home from work early the next day to spend time with the children. It was December 14th. When I walked into the den, there were Louise and Jimmy Ewing and Linda. *Louise has found out, and this is a confrontation,* I immediately thought. I was wrong, thank God! They had stopped by to exchange Christmas gifts. Again, not very cordial, I left the room and went outside to join my children in the backyard, a place at home where I could escape to and immerse myself in the children. The sight of them, happy outside, overwhelmed me. Their laughter was a beautiful sound that simultaneously lifted and crushed my heart. I had to fight back tears. Their spontaneity, their innocence in all that was spiraling around them and their affection for me was so comforting in the midst of all else taking place. I picked them both up, hugging them close and tightly. *God, thank you for this gift, the gift of my children.* They meant the world to me. They were my very life, and I was fearful I could be losing them. Every opportunity I had to repeat this scene, I did, as it was now the only consolation available to me. The nightmare would continue.

When we went back inside, the Ewings had left, mercifully. Linda had put ice cubes in our iced tea glasses. She seemed to want to get dinner over with as quickly as possible, not knowing I did as well. The sooner we were done, the quicker I could assume my usual nightly role with the children, extend that as long as possible before retiring to my bedroom where she and I would not have to endure one another and she could either watch TV alone or get on the phone with that degenerate, when her "family" would be conveniently out of her way.

The wheels of the recorder were turning. It was almost past midnight and the two of them were still on the phone. I had to wait until they had said their goodnights and the recorder stopped advancing before I could assume it safe to listen to the day's recorded conversations.

Linda: "I've got some interesting news."
Ewing: "You're pregnant?"
Linda: "No…but tomorrow Vernon is going out of town. He's going to Columbia. He has a seven o'clock meeting, and he's leaving at five o'clock from here."

I was meeting with Dr. Schnackenberg, the child psychiatrist. This provided the perfect opportunity for the two of them to have a clandestine encounter; and unbeknownst to them, a better opportunity for me to have it all documented.

Linda: "Vernon said he probably wouldn't be back until midnight. So, if you want to drop by for a couple of hours, you're welcome to, like eight o'clock when the kids will be asleep."

She had just invited him to come into our home to indulge in debauchery, while I was away, and one of our children would be sleeping within feet of them. *Had she lost all her couth? Her values?* I thought, *God created attraction, arousal and then, sex for human beings to procreate. That was the intended purpose. Yet some selfishly misuse these functions to the detriment of all others in their sphere of life.*

Ewing: "Reckon it's a trap?"
Linda: "Do you think so?"
Ewing: "Might be."
Linda: That's what I was thinking, too. I don't know. What I could do is around five o'clock I could call his office and talk to Toni, his secretary, and confirm with her his appointment in Columbia; to make sure it's a real appointment. If you came the back way, there'd be no way he would know there's anybody here, with him coming in the side door."
Ewing: "Which he might do."
Linda: "Well, I can deadbolt that side door - which we do every night and that would slow him down on entering. That would give you time to get out. We'll have to be careful anyway in case you have to make a quick exit. You know, you can't be naked. Rhoda is liable to tell me I had a streaker in my backyard last night."

Linda's crude side was on full display. I think that part of her personality had been suppressed during our marriage, and Jimmy Ewing, being the disgusting human being he was, just plain brought out the worst in her. Hearing this conversation and witnessing her total disregard for all she and I had built together, including the children, strengthened my resolve to get through the next few days and, in fact, however long it might take.

Ewing: "I just hate to take a chance on getting you in trouble."

DECEIT

Linda: "Then, why don't I get a babysitter and we could meet somewhere else? Susan said she would sit for us."
Ewing: "Yeah …I'm not sure I want him walking in on us."
Linda: "That's true."
Ewing: "Find me a hiding place in case he walks in on us."

They both laughed.

Linda: "You can always go into my closet in the bedroom. He never goes in there."
Ewing: "Yes, and then I could spend the night with you and ease out mid-morning sometime."

It gave me some solace to know that with every recorded conversation, the lethal legal noose was tightening around both their necks. The detectives were employed full time. Charles Ray would pull that noose tighter with each incident.

Ewing: "You know, I wouldn't be embarrassed if I got caught in bed with you."
Linda: "I know, but it would be bad."
Ewing: "It's going to be bad one of these days anyway you cut it. I think he'd rather be told, than to see it…. You know? If you think it would be safe at your house, we'll just go ahead there. It would be more convenient. He'd probably hear about the babysitter anyway."
Linda: "You could always jump out the bathroom window, Jimmy."
Ewing: "We could make a cozy little fire in the fireplace, and we could roast some marshmallows. As luck might have it, I'll probably get busy with four patients in labor."

Then, Linda joined him at his base, depraved level, in stunning fashion.

Linda: "Just tie their knees together, Jimmy, and tell them they'll have to wait till tomorrow."
Ewing: "You start this weekend, right?"
Linda: "My menstruation?"
Ewing: "Yeah."
Linda: "It's about the third day, I think, or the second."
Ewing: "So, you ought to be safe this month then?"
Linda: I don't know why I should be worried anyway."
Ewing: "Why?"
Linda: "You know why."
Ewing: "That would not stop me. Just teasing you a bit…Go find yourself a big shooter, so it'll run all down your legs. You gonna let Vernon know you're on the pill?"
Linda: "No, he doesn't need to know."
Ewing: "Don't throw away your diaphragm yet."
Linda: "No?"
Ewing: "I imagine you'll want to try him a few more times before you throw him out."

He was prodding her; almost taunting her. Our culture in America gives incredible power to medical doctors. Experiencing that power, Ewing had clearly learned evil ways to use it over the targets of his sex drive.

Linda: "Try him a few more times?"
Ewing: "Between you and him, I don't care."
Linda: "You know I really don't like being on these pills."
Ewing: "Why?"
Linda: "They worry me."
Ewing: "You're just a worry wart."

DECEIT

    Linda had a difficult time during our marriage while on the pill with swollen legs, pain, and the possibility of clotting, so she had switched to a diaphragm.

Ewing: "They're not bothering you now, are they?"
Linda: "Yes, one leg is aching more than the other. And I've been waking up in the middle of the night with the muscles of my legs wanting to cramp. I used to have these same pains, the muscles wanting to cramp at night, especially when I was pregnant."
Ewing: "Maybe so."
Linda: "I'll take them for a while. I'll see how I do."
Ewing: "I hope things work out tomorrow."
Linda: "Me, too. I'm thinking we should just meet here. It would be more comfortable. Nicer."
Ewing: "You checked out the path lately?"

    He was referring to the alleyway behind our property and each of the houses on the block. The alleyway extended behind the houses throughout the entire neighborhood.

Linda: "It's all right. The only thing is the West's have that bright light out there. It's lit up pretty much all the time. Once you pass the Wests, then you're back behind my house and, of course, we have high shrubs and so do the Browns. I could meet you out there and, of course, my backyard is dark."

    There I was, sitting in the closet of the house my wife and I had built for the sincere, God-given pleasure for us to share life and care for one of God's greatest gifts in life: children. Now this very same structure had become a house of horror, delivering a different kind of pleasure, a primitive, instinctual kind of pleasure; a pleasure empty of higher mindedness fueled by a sick drive that destroys everything in its path, seemingly even the two participants' own deeper human needs. The peace and security of fragile innocent children, the intended beneficiaries of this home's original design, was headed toward destruction!

CHAPTER SEVEN

The next morning I tried to concentrate on business, which was impossible as I was preoccupied with the knowledge that Ewing would be in my home that evening while the children slept nearby. It was Friday, December 15th, a week and a half since my revelation. Knowing I'd be leaving for Columbia late in the afternoon for the appointment with Dr. Schnackenberg, I went home early afternoon to spend time with the children. We stayed outside most of the time, to avoid interaction with Linda. During my precious time spent with the little ones, I tried to block out, as best I could, visions of what would occur that evening in my absence. Linda was in the house doing the typical chores she had done for years in happier times, but now with new and exciting adventures swirling around in her head and heart. She was only waiting for my absence to put her plans into action.

I set out for Columbia at five o'clock. For two hours en route, my mind reverberated with the conversations I'd heard, fighting back tears for a portion of the trip. It was killing me knowing what would occur in my home with my children close by while I was driving 100 miles west in the opposite direction. *This should be something I should be stopping, not purposely permitting*, I thought. But, it had to be done, so I kept my foot on the accelerator. Along the way, I passed homes with Christmas decorations outside and inside. These were homes occupied, I imagined, by people who upheld principles, who spoke truth, who practiced delayed gratification, and who truly cared for their family members. My home had lost these attributes.

My stomach's role was no longer solely food digestion. It was now also a cruel furnace where flames went forth into every cell in my body that had held trust and faith in the power of love and in truth spoken by loved ones. But that trust and faith were history. As I experienced this roasting alive, this night, I could hear catcalls and snickers from my home, from the stairs, from Linda's bedroom, from the Christmas tree in the den, and from the roaring fireplace I knew was providing comfort and solace that evening to the two adulterers in this sordid tale. After the holidays, I'd be ordered out of the house. It would be easier for Ewing to get to her after we were separated, and I was no longer around to interfere.

Letting my instinctual desires take flight, I thought of Ewing being dragged out of the house and through the streets of town on his face against the concrete while someone with a bullhorn announced, "Here's what we think of this scumbag of a human being who calls himself a doctor; as we dump his limp, lifeless, stinking carcass into the street sewer."

In Columbia at his office, Dr. Schnackenberg greeted me warmly. Instantly, I felt like I had a friend - he was that kind of guy; sympathetic, empathetic, and very understanding. I recounted to him everything that had happened; my wife was in the midst of an affair with her doctor, the man who had delivered our baby girl; her plan to remove me from the house; the wiretap and its contents, my association with attorney Jan Warner and the detectives; and most importantly, my absolute need to gain custody of my two children because of the abuse they had endured and the kind of man she intended to have as their full-time parent. Dr. Schnackenberg was rapt with interest in my situation and seemed to care deeply for the welfare of the children. With concern and urgency in his voice, he advised me to return with the children and he made appointments for us for the 29th of December and January 3rd.

On the way back to Florence I stopped at a phone booth to call Charles Ray to learn about the evening's surveillance. He and his associate had taken their positions at 5:30 p.m. at the back of the house where they could easily observe Linda through the rear windows. Learning for the first time, as it turned out, the neighbor behind our home had gone through a similar domestic experience and, coincidentally, Charles Ray was the detective in that case as well. Charles' favorable relationship with that neighbor worked greatly to our advantage when Charles made arrangements to set up their reconnaissance positions in the neighbor's backyard. By elevating themselves in that backyard, Ray and his colleague were able to see directly into our home through the bay windows in the dining area and the large plate glass window of our den. They could see Linda serving David and Jade their dinner. *At* 6:10, Charles Ray noted that my wife exited the house, went to the woodpile, and filled up her arms with as much wood as she could carry. Returning to the house, she went back inside to the fireplace.

At 7:10, all the outside lights of the house went on and she emerged again, walking back and forth in the yard, as if she might be waiting for someone. Then, she went back inside, where she was seen answering the phone. It was 7:35 p.m. She turned off all the outside lights and came out onto the back doorsteps. At this time, a man was observed walking down the alleyway behind and between the backyards of the properties in the block. He stopped at the gate that led into our backyard and, opening the gate, he proceeded to the back steps where, Ray said, Mrs. Baumrind and the man embraced and then, entered the house. The detectives observed smoke drifting out of the chimney.

With binoculars, Ray and his partner observed the couple, who had entered the house in front of the fireplace, lying on the carpeted floor unclothed from the waist down. They were able to identify the couple as Mrs. Baumrind and Dr. James Ewing. At 9:35, both Mrs. Baumrind and Dr. Ewing exited the house from the back door. She accompanied him to the rear gate. She watched him as he walked into the alleyway, and she went back into the house. I was numb from this account. While the detective was amused at his accomplishments, I was unable to share his enthusiasm; but I knew this was another episode of documented debauchery that would serve me well in court later.

I wondered how much longer this had to go on and how much lower would my wife stoop. I didn't yet know that before this was all over, she would descend almost to the doctor's lowest level. She had orchestrated this bawdy event without any consideration for the sanctity of our home. And she would hatch several more of these trysts before this Christmas season ended. My heart was devastated; I couldn't get used to this new norm.

I returned home after midnight. The children were snug in their beds. Linda was in her room with the door closed. Even the Christmas tree seemed to know what had happened in our beautiful home that evening that we had built together for our family. I avoided the spot where I knew they would have positioned themselves on the floor in front of the fireplace, glancing at it in disgust as I walked by on my way upstairs to my quarters.

Several conversations from the day were recorded, followed by their conversation subsequent to that evening's event.

Linda: "You made it home okay?"
Ewing: "Yeah. I enjoyed it."
Linda: "Yeah, too bad it had to be so nerve-wracking. I think it would have been better if we had gone to your office."
Ewing: "At least we could have relaxed."
Linda: "Yes, that's what I meant…maybe when he's a little further away, it'll be easier. You know, knowing that he's not going to be back that night."

Now she was mimicking him; the student was mirroring the teacher - the easiest way to get the lesson correct.

Ewing: "Sure is a pretty house you've got."
Linda: "I designed the inside of it."

As if I didn't have enough to be incensed about, now she was taking full credit for the interior décor, when in fact we'd collaborated on it from beginning to end!

Ewing: "Hate you'll have to give it up."
Linda: "Yeah."
Ewing: "That's what you get for sin. Looks like what I've taken is what he wanted…do you know what he's thinking?"

Linda: "No, I don't know. Sometimes I think he knows and other times I think, no, he doesn't. But he didn't say anything tonight to make me think he suspected."
Ewing: "He didn't?"
Linda: "Not one thing, unless he can hide it that well."
Linda: "It's going to be a traumatic thing; and I'm sure the first several weeks will be bad on me, you know, when we separate, with the children asking questions and all."

 That the children would "ask questions" was the depth of her concern for them? How shallow! There was zero concern for how devastating divorce would be or how imperiled the children could be when exposed to daily life with a compulsive sex addict. She displayed no hint of compassion for the husband she knew loved her for all these years and no concern shown for how the children might feel about their father being expelled from the house and from their lives. *Heartless*, I thought. Driven by her own carnality and sexual obsession now, led by a savant in those areas, Linda's blind spot had rewritten her inner moral code.

 Then there was a discussion on the wisdom of her immediately setting up an individual bank account, changing the locks on the house, and setting up new rules I would have to follow.

Ewing: "The main thing is you just don't want him to come and go as he pleases. And you, in particular, don't want him coming in when you've got somebody there. You'll need to get his keys to the house, till you can change the locks… Hey! When he came home last night, did he say he thought there was too much red pubic hair on your rug in front of the fireplace?" [They both laughed.]

CHAPTER EIGHT

Tension continued to build, an unseen pressure, growing more powerful each day, like a poison gas that had begun to choke the very air I breathed. It was December 16th, another day in the middle of this nightmare with no end in sight. This day was no easier than any other, trying to keep up with my business, knowing what had gone on in my home. Could I hold myself together until Jan Warner would tell me we had enough evidence? Could I avoid doing something irrational that would jeopardize all that had been accomplished over the past couple of weeks? Could I continue my theatrical performance? My acting was a lie in the face of their lies. And the battle of lies was in full tilt.

I left the office early again and went back home to be with David and Jade. I stayed in the house only momentarily before I took their hands and got them outside into the fresh air. I took them down to the park by the neighborhood church and we played hide and seek, crawling through the concrete pipes again and hiding behind bushes until it began to grow dark early in the late winter afternoon, and it was time to return home.

Linda had dinner ready. We said nothing to each other since I'd come home. If you'd touched that silence between us, you'd have gotten electrocuted.

Just as we were ready to sit down, David began to tease Jade. "Jade's a dumb boy, Jade's a dumb boy!" he chanted repeatedly.

Linda lost it. She reached out and struck him squarely across the face. He reeled back in shock, pain, and surprise—my own shock equal to his. I jumped up to protect him and swung my arm to push her out of the way, but instead I struck her arm.

"Keep your hands off him!" I yelled. I grabbed David, who was crying, and held him in my arms, but I also felt bad about striking Linda and said, "Linda, God, I'm sorry. This is too much to deal with." Like a volcano about to erupt, I was coming close to unraveling and blurting out all my frustration, but I bit my tongue - again. The act had to go on.

Now Jade was crying. I took David into the bathroom to wash him up. I would not allow her to abuse the children. No matter what went on between us, I wouldn't tolerate any more abuse - physical or otherwise - and there had been some.

I put David's toys in the tub and Linda brought Jade in. I put Jade in the tub too, and soon the bath and the fact that they were children seemed to eclipse what had just taken place. They played together happily as if nothing had happened. How were they to know? They had no idea. I still had to continue with this masquerade, but I had to do a better job of containing myself and controlling my emotions.

After I got them each tucked in and whispered goodnight, I stood there and looked down at them. There was nothing left to do now but to go to my room and repeat the process that had become routine - listening to the daily recordings. I thought, *How sick and sad is that?* I had to wait an hour for Linda to get off the phone, and then I turned on the tape recorder.

Ewing: "Do you know how much birdbaths cost?"
Linda: "Well, when I bought mine, I think they were around twenty-five to thirty dollars. They might be up to fifty dollars now."
Ewing: "I thought they were more than that. I want to get one for Louise. Wish you could go shopping with me. Would you like that?"

    I hadn't ever thought that there would come a time in my life when I would be sitting in a closet of my own house, banished there by my wife, while she talked on the telephone to her lover about the price of birdbaths. But birdbaths were nothing compared to the topic next on their agenda.

Ewing: "You did good last night. Who've you been practicing on? You been doing that for Vernon?"
Linda: "No."
Ewing: "Must have been the mailman....'cause you did good. Practice makes perfect! It makes me feel really good to know that you try to please me."
Linda: "Well, I want to and that's why I do it. Or I'm trying to."
Ewing: "Did it go better last night? Did you try to gulp it down as soon as you could?"
Linda: "Well, I kept it in the back like you told me to."
Ewing: "With all this weird food you eat, you have trouble stomaching that?"
Linda: "Yes."
Ewing: "I believe it's all in your head."
Linda: "Wherever it is, it's hard. You don't have any patients this afternoon, do you?"
Ewing: "Just got that one in labor."

Birdbaths one minute, oral sex another, then, births of babies the next.

Ewing: "Hope I didn't upset you with all of my talk last night."
Linda: "Well, to be honest, you did. You said you need to be with other women at least a couple of times each year. I did a little arithmetic. That comes out to about sixty."
Ewing: "About sixty?"
Linda: "Yes. In thirty years."
Ewing: "It's just natural for me to be attracted to other people."
Linda: "But you need some self-restraint too."
Ewing: "I've got a little."
Linda: "Gee, that's not very encouraging."
Ewing: "It's just an ego thing to get seduced by another woman. I'm sure I'd be tempted a couple of times a year to see somebody else. That's about the way it has worked out so far. I'm just human, you know. It's only because I've been unhappy and lonely. Maybe you just don't believe me?"
Linda: "No, I believe you."
Ewing: "Well, I don't know if I could turn down an opportunity if there is a chance. But I don't have any other designs. It's just a real strong ego thing. Nobody's perfect. I might slip up and make a mistake every now and then. You might too. I'm sure you are attracted to other people too. Get a little too much wine on board one night and you might take on somebody, you know. Those things happen."

Linda: "But, it should be different when you're married to someone you love and he's supposed to love you, but he's going out on the side."

So, let's see, I thought, *…it's OK for her to go outside her current marriage for sex, but not OK for her proposed partner to go outside his marriage to her. Right! So, how do we make sense of this twisted logic? Her brief dissertation on loyalty reveals her irrational thinking about her own morals.*

Ewing: "Well, I might slow down a little as I get older… But, you know, it's an ego thing to have women seduce you. What about you? You might start getting itchy yourself after you get tired of me. Why are you getting so upset? All I said was that I didn't know if I could turn down a threesome if I had the chance. You sound so upset about it. You're over-reacting. You're not getting emotional, are you?"
Linda: "I guess I've just never been faced with all this before. It's kind of hard for me to accept."

I could hear Linda quieting the children in the background so that she could hear their telephone conversation. Her upside-down priorities were on full display this day.

Ewing: "A lot of men, they've had hundreds of women. A couple of different ones every week."

All of this to give himself license to do the same, I thought. And the compulsive one was leading the obsessive one to his higher level of sickness.

Ewing: "Want me to line you up?"

Linda: "No."

Ewing: "It's nothing more than what we see in the movies these days."

Linda: "Yeah, you like to watch X-rated movies. And you're showing them to me now."

Ewing: "I used to watch all the time…I think I'm going to order a couple for us."

Linda: "Oh, my."

Ewing: "You going to begrudge me one little threesome with you?"

Linda: "With me…I don't know how you'd want to go about it…First, one girl, then the other? Is that what you'd want, Jimmy?"

Ewing: "Well, you know, in the middle of it all…it's just one of those ego things. To believe it enough, I'm a good enough lover to take care of several women at the same time…And we're not going to just get some hooker off the street…And it might not be a question of first or second. It might be a question of first, second, third, fourth and fifth."

Ewing kept taunting her, daring her to be outraged by his notions. All of a sudden, it was all making sense to me. Movies! X-rated movies! This guy's sex addiction had consumed him by its psychological, emotional, and physiological power. Why hadn't that been obvious to me earlier? Why would this not have been obvious to Linda? His obsession with sex had long ago morphed from obsession to compulsive sexual behavior to including partners and porn. The combination of the two created the current drive that directed every conversation back to sex. He was consumed. He needed more and more of this and needed it more frequently. Under the control of his addiction, he spoke as he thought and acted accordingly. Linda was no match to this force, or his high intellect twisted to fit his drive. My horror grew as I realized that everyone whose life is touched by this man has the inescapable potential to become a victim of his obsessions. His entire mindset evolved around instant sexual gratification. It was Linda's responsibility as a mother and my wife to recognize this behavior and to deal with it responsibly. She did not! If she had any semblance of a conscience, she was ignoring it. She had become a facilitator; an enabler. And everyone in her family would suffer the long-term consequences of his behavior along with her.

Ewing: "You don't think I would do you just once, do you?"
Linda: "I don't know what you have in mind, Jimmy."
Ewing: "It's just such a big turn-on having two girls licking my cock at the same time, taking turns getting them off. It's a strong feeling. You've seen it now, you know, in the movies. Louise says she would do it with us. Would you do it with us?"

    In breathtakingly sick style, Ewing's first mention of his wife in these fantasies of his implied she knew of his escapades with Linda. Or was it a lie to encourage Linda's participation in a threesome; just another instance of manipulation?

Linda: "No, I don't think so. She lies a lot though."
Ewing: "No, she meant it."
Linda: "Maybe because she knows I won't."
Ewing: "You wouldn't with her? If you'd do it, I'd enjoy you more. You can make her swallow it....You think I'm bad, don't you? Are you ashamed of it?"

He seemed to be seeking affirmation of his brashness; his calling card, with shock and awe as his desired response—all-the-while manipulating her, moving her along the path he intended.

Linda: "No, I guess I'm just not liberal enough. I don't know, you might like it and want me to do it more."
Ewing: "You might like it too."
Linda: "No, I don't think I would want to watch you enjoy somebody else."
Ewing: "Won't you?"
Linda: "I'm too conservative."

But she wasn't conservative enough to uphold the basic principles that rule out sex with one's gynecologist. Her words were part of the steady flow, each of them symptoms of a conscience ignored.

Ewing: "Would you rather me get with two different women? I really mean it. I'd enjoy you more if you would. You'd be more real, more loving, if you'd do it."
Linda: "It would be too embarrassing."
Ewing: "Would you rather me have another woman instead of you?"
Linda: "No, I don't want that either."
Ewing: "Would it be embarrassing to see somebody else watch you suck my cock?"
Linda: "Yeah."
Ewing: "Wouldn't you enjoy seeing someone else suck my cock?"
Linda: "No, I guess I'm just not liberal enough. Let's not talk about it anymore."

He had a stunning lack of conscience and no morals. This "Bad Boy" did naughty things. He knew what he wanted and there was no deterring him. She was attracted to his persona, had fallen for him, and lowered herself to his level, sliding down the moral scale with him. Nothing was going to stop either one of them from what they wanted for themselves. Whatever her life was prior to this, it was history. In shock and disbelief, I knew I had to recognize the reality of what was occurring. I simply didn't measure up any longer; and neither did the children."

Ewing: "You sound so upset about it. You're over-reacting. You're not getting emotional, are you?"
Linda: "Yeah, 'cause I'm upset."
Ewing: "I just don't understand why you're upset. I told you I only need this occasionally, I'm human. It's just natural for me."

Human, I thought. *This sounds more natural for an animal's conduct. Farm animals think at higher levels than this!*

Linda: "Let's not talk about it anymore."
Ewing: "I really don't think I would keep seeing other women if I was happily married. You know already I stopped seeing Jane when you and I started seeing one another regularly."
Linda: "I really don't think you would either, but that still upsets me."
Ewing: "Well, that's all I can say, Linda."
Linda: "Yeah, I know, so, we don't have to talk about it anymore."
Ewing: "You're just going to continue being upset."
Linda: "No, I'll get over it."

Ewing: "You're not going to find anybody that's perfect."
Linda: "Yeah. I know. Well, maybe I'd better let you go and get your lunch?"
Ewing: "You still upset?"
Linda: "I don't know. I'll have to see when I get off the phone."

Had Ewing bumped into Linda's subdued conscience, her moral compass? To him, he'd found another barrier to break through; another challenge, a wall to tear down. But his manipulation would prevail!

Ewing: "We can't be happy if you stay upset all the time worrying about something that might possibly happen somewhere down the way. As you know, I was never happy with Louise in bed, and then I discovered and enjoyed somebody else, what somebody else had…Would you do it?"
Linda: "No, I don't think so."
Ewing: "You know what I think?"
Linda: "What?"
Ewing: "I think you're just looking for reasons to reject me."
Linda: "No."
Ewing: "Trying to convince yourself you ought to stay where you are and forget about me. I think you're just going out of your way to try to find fault."
Linda: "I don't' know, maybe I'm being too idealistic."
Ewing: "I've got some good points, but don't get the idea I'm perfect, you see."
Linda: "Well, I'm not either."
Ewing: "You'd better be. You have to take some chances in life or, if not, you stay where you are and count your

blessings. You're making an awful lot over something that might not ever be a problem."

Ewing's strawman suggestion of "stay where you are and count your blessings" was a valid opportunity for Linda. But, for her, taking a healthy, principled path to an enjoyable life had ended, apparently months ago, at the fork in the road where her "Bad Boy" showed up, where she ignored her conscience in favor of an alternative definition of "enjoyable." By now, this path was foregone.

Linda: "Well, I'm thinking too. I don't know - you seem to want somebody that's ready for sex on command."
Ewing: "You are."
Linda: "No, I'm not."
Ewing: "Every time I've been with you."
Linda: "Well, I make myself that way for you, but I'm not always sexy. I'd better go. I have to put Jade to bed. It's past her nap time. I'll be all right. I'm not trying to reject you."
Ewing: "Yes, you are."
Linda: "I know. You always know what you have, but you don't know what you are going to get and get yourself into."

This was a foreboding observation, I thought.

Ewing: "Maybe you ought to just keep what you've got. If you expect me to be perfect, you're going to be disappointed."
Linda: "No, I don't expect you to be perfect!"

The tape had advanced to its end. I turned it off and tried to clear my mind of their voices. I realized that I had actually gotten involved with these two tacky, outlandish, desperate people as though I didn't even know them but as characters in a soap opera you could not watch - ones you hated, ones you loved. But I had no choice. I had to watch this disgusting drama.

I could see his use of emotional leverage on Linda by indirection and suggestion, as he manipulated her feelings for him and his insatiable appetite for sex; making her feel responsible for his emotions and needs. He may have even been getting a perverted sexual kick out of her being upset with all this talk. I wasn't sure. He never promised her anything - only exploited her feelings to gratify himself. His conversations were filled with sexual innuendo and graphic suggestions. Linda had become more and more complicit; and at the same time, she seemed to be seeing in him what she wanted to see, not what actually existed, and she was oblivious to his manipulation. Her own lack of self-esteem had turned her into the perfect prey for this arrogant beast's daily appetite for power and sex. She had fully submitted herself to him.

In listening to Ewing's disgusting telephone conversations, there was so much I wanted to say to Linda. I wanted her to see through his manipulative conversations and her protestations of affection for him that were never returned, to make her more aware of how often he turned her conversations around to discussions of sexual play, in spite of her evident discomfort. My own emotions were vacillating. I felt for her in one moment and then, in another, I was disgusted with her. I still can't explain my feelings - why I would be sympathetic for her, but I was. I wanted to take and shield her from him, to hold her close to me. But I had been cast out and she wouldn't care what I wanted for her. She had made her choice—him! Her moral compass had descended to a point of no return.

I began to understand a little better what had happened between Linda and me. This man's influence on her was so overpowering that once his control was established, there was no breaking that grasp. This had happened months ago. My every good intention was misconstrued. My compulsion to try to reach her, my expressions of feelings for her, my pathetic pleadings weeks ago were met with an equal display of dispassion. She was already detached from me in October and November, or perhaps earlier. The emotional bond had been broken; and I just hadn't understood that.

If she would expose herself to a crass, foul-mouthed, sleazy character who had no morals and talked as he did to her, then my children would also ultimately be exposed to this kind of behavior. He would manipulate them as he was manipulating her. The children should never come under his influence. His conversations were not that of the highly principled professional he professed to be. Beneath that respectable façade lay a shabby, unethical, egotistical womanizer. He didn't possess the character to commit to his own family and wife and he surely wouldn't feel any more responsibility to mine. These were two married people, not married to each other; each cheating and deceiving their respective families. Both were dishonest. The children should never get the idea that this behavior is acceptable.

"Why wiretap the extension phone?" I would be asked in litigation, as though my having done that was such a terrible thing and I should be ashamed of what I had done. Had I not recorded, would anyone believe what I was hearing? Not likely. I was the offended husband. It would be assumed I was conjuring all this up; all in my mind, for how it might advantage me. The wiretap was validation as well as my salvation. The contents of the wiretap were and have always been indisputable. I had to continue to subject myself to this garbage, this desecration. I was in the process of forging the unspeakable - taking our children away from their mother—and every incident with this perverted sex deviant would be damaging to her. Still, the norm is for children to go with the mother. My fear was that that was non-negotiable. I took a deep breath and turned the recorder back on.

Ewing: "You got company?"
Linda: "No."
Ewing: "You upset?"
Linda: "It started when I got angry with David, and I slapped him and Vernon turned around and hit me in the arm, just grazed me."
Ewing: "Did he hurt you? Has he ever done that before?"
Linda: "No, never. He didn't really hurt me. He said that I've made it perfectly clear that there's nothing left between us…and he said it was all over and there's no feeling left for him either. He said I've made it easier for him…and that he's had enough. That was pretty much it. He didn't say anything about you, and I sort of asked him, 'what do you mean, I've done enough?' He didn't say anything else. He just said he was locking up and went upstairs."

Right! I wasn't going to be drawn out by responding to her question. She could have gotten her intended response from me, but it was not time yet.

DECEIT

Out in the winter night I could hear Christmas carols coming from a neighbor, the Martins' house. Every year at this time they had carols playing for all of us to hear. "Silent Night" was drifting out now. Such tranquility in the singers' voices sounded angelic but ironic for all that was occurring in my home. For a polar opposite to "Silent Night," I returned to the day's recording.

Ewing: "I'm sorry."
Linda: "Well, I guess it's separation and then divorce."
Ewing: "I'm sorry he hit you. Don't you usually discipline the children?"
Linda: "Yes."
Ewing: "You don't sound too good."
Linda: "I'm all right. I was all right until you called, and I heard your voice…and I got all upset."
Ewing: "You sound awful."
Linda: "I knew it would come to this. He's right. I've pretty much brought all this about. He might be an understanding person, but I've never pushed him this far. He's got a right to be upset. I was thinking tonight after he went upstairs to bed, 'I sure am glad I'm the woman and not the man. It would kill me to lose the children.' That's what he's feeling."
Ewing: "Well, I did try to draw y'all apart. But maybe it's just a bad case of fuckingitis."

This guy is a real healer, I thought. Both of these people were devoid of compassion, even for one another.

Linda made no comment and the rest of the tape had to do with whether they could make arrangements to get to one another at his office the next afternoon. I again listened to the sound of the Christmas carols, this time filling my mind as better memories might and soothing the darkness around me. Then, I went into each child's bedroom to look into their faces before returning to my assigned spot in the house. I was still not totally confident in the outcome of all this and in fear for their futures should I not be successful in my efforts.

    I kept repeating to myself, to buoy my resolve, *They'll never catch us…they'll never catch us.*

CHAPTER NINE

A week passed. It was Saturday, December 23rd, Linda's and my eleventh wedding anniversary, and Linda would see Ewing twice this day before the sun went down. I left the house with the children at around 9:30 and returned at 12:30. I went upstairs and checked the tape. "I'll come," Linda told Ewing, "See you in about fifteen minutes."

She had gone to him and came tearing in at about 12:55, then rushed a lunch together. Because she was late for lunch, the kids were cranky, which made me restless, so I left the room until Linda called us to the table. After lunch she left quickly, saying that she had more shopping she wanted to do for Christmas. I offered no comment.

As soon as she left, I called Charles Ray and asked him whether he'd had her under surveillance this morning and was pleased to learn that he had. He said that fifteen minutes after I'd left the house with the kids, she drove off in her car and went directly to the Medical Center Building and entered Ewing's office. She was seen to leave at 12:10. No one else was seen entering Ewing's office during this time. I didn't know it yet, but this torturous experience was coming to a close quicker than I'd thought possible, at least the first phase of it.

In case the tapes were not going to be allowed in the domestic issue or at trial, which was certainly a possibility,

I was not to breathe a word of the existence of any tape recordings. We did not know yet about the legality of the wiretap, but at least now Charles Ray was documenting everything at his discretion, full time.

    I left the house at 2:30 to take the children to the movies and we returned at 4:45. Linda was home, and I immediately drove to the corner service station where I called Charles again to learn what he had observed while the children and I were away. He advised that she had walked down to the Ewing house, where she remained until 4:30.

    When I returned to the house, Linda was in the kitchen and the children were in the playroom. I went upstairs to check the tape.

Linda: "Hi. Tried to call you earlier."
Ewing: "How long ago?"
Linda: "You weren't plugged in. Your answering service was... What are you doing?"
Ewing: "I'm just lying in bed."
Linda: "You going to take a nap?"
Ewing: "No. I just took a bath."
Linda: "Oh."
Ewing: "You got me all dirty. Smelly. I didn't know whether you were going to come near me this morning or not."
Linda: "You were fine."
Ewing: "Louise has gone shopping somewhere. She said she probably wouldn't be back until 4 o'clock… You could naively drop by, just to look at our tree or something."
Linda: "Oh dear. She's liable to come back early."
Ewing: "It's up to you."

Linda: "You know I'd like to see you. It's just that I'm afraid."
Ewing: "Don't you ever drop by without calling?"
Linda: "Yeah, I do. Especially since your kids aren't there, I guess I could come. Where are your kids?"
Ewing: "Wade is skating and Victoria is somewhere. She's just liable to come back. I don't want you to get in a compromised situation. But I'm comfortable doing it."
Linda: "No, I'll come. I'll walk down. Bye."

    I was still struggling with opposing emotions and desires and conflicted by strong feelings for the importance of family and the hope, however remote it may have been, that Linda would have an epiphany, reverse herself, and take a path to salvaging her family. This surely would have been a colossal undertaking on my part, but I had to leave the door open for the possibility. Did she have any semblance of decency? Was she capable of a genuine attempt at authenticity? That possibility seemed more remote than ever now.

    The following day, Christmas Eve, I tried again to see if she could put her family above herself. This would not be my last attempt. We had always enjoyed bike riding, and when I suggested it, she nodded affirmatively. David rode his tricycle and Jade rode in the carrier on the back of my bike. We actually looked like a family again - the perfect family - all of us peddling out into the neighborhood. It was a pleasant and relatively warm December afternoon. The illusion of a happy family did not last long. My heart was still heavy with the facts swirling around in my head. As we headed home, Ewing and his wife approached us from up the street. They were between us and our home. There was no way to avoid them. As we drew nearer, I looked at his face, glanced at her, then looked back at him. It was obvious they had exchanged unspoken messages.

    Emotions welled up within me. In an instant all hell could have broken loose. Every muscle in my body trembled. I wanted to tear him to pieces right there in the middle of the street of our neighborhood, where both of us were well known. He wouldn't have stood a chance with the profusion of adrenaline that was pumping through my veins. But the next day's headlines would read: "Neighbor Pummels Neighbor to Death in Street for No Reason" and their affair would go undetected without the evidence that was needed yet. I focused on the children and my wiser-self prevailed. We exchanged pleasantries and passed one another like proverbial passing ships in the night.

    The next day was Christmas; the most miserable Christmas of my life - a day to just get through. I was tired the moment I got up. The children were excited about their presents though, and after breakfast we set out for Christmas dinner at my parent's home.

    We should have stayed home. We were unable to conceal the tension and the day was absolutely ruined for everyone. I found an opportunity to advise my parents very briefly on what was going on, so they would understand the tension. They were supportive and offered to help in any way possible, understanding that a custody battle lay ahead.

    We left my parents' house early and drove back to Florence to our non-house, our non-home, our non-hearth, to her bed, to mine. There was one last Christmas present awaiting me at bedtime - there would be no tapes to listen to this day. Merry Christmas!

CHAPTER TEN

It was Thursday, December 28th. Their conversations, two a day, three, sometimes four, spun in my head like a tape reel gone mad, faster, faster, faster.

Linda: "Hi!"
Ewing: "Hi! Where's Hickey?"
Linda: "Gone."
Ewing: "I was wanting to come check you out last night, especially since you're so juicy and everything and I've thought about screwing you all day today. By the way, care for a little fuck? Have you been playing with it anymore?"

The man was depraved. Depravity goes beyond mere bad behavior. It is a condition of mind, heart, and soul. It is a complete lack of morals, values, and even regard for other living things, like the depravity of a serial killer. But an out-of-control sex addict's victims experience a different kind of death—a slow torture of self-devaluation, the end of a dreamed life for us all, and children left without the security of having two parents.

Linda: "Okay! Let's not get into that!"
Ewing: "You were trying to save it for me today, huh?"

Linda: "Yes, I was all ready for you today."
Ewing: "I wanted you to come to the office today where I could sneak you in the back door and inspect my cherry. Would you like that?"
Linda: "Stop it!"
Ewing: "I want you to like it.

    Over and over and over! He had fanned her desire into a consuming passion. In his image, she had become a sex maniac. But here the teacher's student was pushing back. Consumed by his own untethered juggernaut sex drive, Ewing was bumping against the remaining fragment of Linda's moral code. Lacking as it was, her morality dangling by a thread, but clearly not enough to do an about face from her treachery, I had almost lost all hope for that.

    I mused to myself about how certain people in society, especially doctors, are expected to be virtuous. But this man, a gynecologist, was operating beyond the norms of right and wrong, under his own rules to maximize his insatiable appetite for sex with vulnerable patients who could be exploited. Among them, dreadfully, my wife. I would eventually learn that she was but one of many; that this behavior was habitual with this guy. His telephone conversations with selected patients were loaded with lewd suggestive comments, vulgarities, sexual innuendos, and graphic off-colored jokes. He represents the height of hypocrisy, an insatiable seeker of pleasure, a man who professes one way through the facade of his title, doctor, behaving like Clark Kent when in public, and like a lewd, perverted super-creep when he is alone with a woman. I'm not making excuses for Linda because she, too, had character deficiencies, but she was no match to his exploitative, dominating behavior. In fact, her passivity and compliance made her the perfect partner for his perverted, commanding persona. He sought to subvert her, to manipulate her into feeling responsible for his sexual and emotional needs. He would tell her what he wanted her to do, and if she was hesitant or repulsed about something, he would tell her, "I would enjoy you more, if you would," thus, using emotional leverage to get her to satisfy his perversions. And she accommodated.

And this was the man who was going to replace me in the lives of my children! It was not going to happen. I was determined, somehow, someway, to prevail.

It was 6:30 a.m. after another sleepless night. In a daze, I showered and dressed. Before leaving for the office, I had to try one last desperate time to get through to her—for our family. I had to give her the opportunity for one last offramp, though I had no idea how, if she had relented, that I could ever live with her with the vivid recollections of all I had heard and all that had occurred.

I entered her bedroom and sat down on the edge of her bed. She woke slowly. I said to her, "Linda, we've been together thirteen years now and have every good reason, especially with our two children, to save our family. This is the last time I will ask you to work with me on the issues, whatever they are. I want to understand why you are unhappy. I want to resolve any problems. When I fell in love with you, it was forever and that hasn't changed in all this time."

She understood what I was saying, but her mind was clearly made up. Her interests were elsewhere. She responded, "I just don't love you anymore and we need to separate."

That was it. It was over. The curtain had closed. The End. I rose slowly and walked out.

Later that day, she related the incident to Ewing:

Linda: "Guess what he just did this morning? He came into my bedroom and sat on the edge of the bed and asked if we could work on our problems for our family's sake."
Ewing: "And…?"
Linda: "So, I said we just need to separate…I don't love you anymore. What do you think about that, Jimmy? Do you think I'm crazy?" [she laughs.]

The height of her insensitivity was beyond my comprehension, and she had become morally bankrupt. My wife had lost all sense of family. She was no longer capable of thinking beyond her immediate indulgence in fleeting pleasures.

Ewing: "I think you're crazy about *me*. Looks like he's by himself on this. Everything will be so much better when he's not around."

Turning on a dime, consistent with their hyperfocus on sexual exploits, their conversation immediately went to their plans to meet the next day when I would be out of town. I was scheduled to take the children to meet Dr. Schnackenberg in Columbia. I had told her I was taking the children to the Columbia zoo. I would do that, of course, and then see Dr. Schnackenberg with the children, in the hope that the children would only report to her the trip to the zoo and nothing else.

Ewing: "Are you sure he's taking the children with him? Do you want to go with them?"
Linda: "I'd rather see you."

As I listened, despair became the air I breathed, and Ewing was an undefeatable monster. Maybe I was hiding behind my children? Was it an honorable thing to do to plot and wrench one's children away from their mother? What kind of man would do this? Answering that question to myself; *One who loves his children more than anything else in this world and is the better, more responsible, and more stable parent.* Family had vacated her mind, heart, and soul. I had no choice but to press on.

Friday, December 29th was the children's appointment day in Columbia with Dr. Schnackenberg. While we would be gone, Linda and Ewing would have free reign to do just about anything they wanted to do unhindered. I already knew from their tape-recorded conversation they planned to meet in a public park that afternoon. It was to be a pivotal experience for them - and for me, as well. Little did they know, they would have company in the park that day.

The children knew this was to be a big day for them, and they were excited during breakfast. I told them I had to first go to work for a little while, but I'd come back home for them, and we'd leave on our trip. When I arrived home about 11:30, Linda had the children ready and had prepared our lunch. We ate and then departed, but not before I looked at her long and meaningfully. *If only all this were not necessary,* I thought.

That now-familiar mixed bag of emotions accompanied me on the drive to Columbia with the children that afternoon. It was great to have this time with them, off alone on an adventure to the zoo and exciting to know they were finally meeting Dr. Schnackenberg, who I expected would be instrumental in giving me the best shot at gaining custody in court. Along with my sadness, I felt an exhilarating sense of pride and wholesomeness as a father on such a noble mission.

David had just turned five the day before. A trip to the zoo for kids five and two-and-a-half was as good as it gets and they enjoyed every minute of the adventure, except for the smell of urine and excrement in the animal enclosures, which seemed to have made the biggest impression on them that day. I knew it would be a good experience for them to discuss with their mother and that that conversation would likely deflect to it from anything else they may have been inclined to discuss with her including the visit with the psychiatrist.

I kept watching the time for our appointment with Dr. Schnackenberg, and we departed the zoo early enough to catch a bite to eat at McDonald's before meeting with the doctor in his office. Even the short visit to McDonalds would be memorable to them—more so than any conversation they may have had that day with an old man who we just happened to bump into incidentally on this adventure to the zoo. Dr. Schnackenberg spent a couple of hours with us; with me initially for a few minutes, while his secretary entertained the children, and then with each child separately.

Following through with their plans, I would later hear on tape, Linda and Ewing met at McLeod Park that afternoon, likely at the same time the children and I were at the zoo and then, McDonalds in Columbia. I had coordinated beforehand with the detectives to document this illicit, adulterous encounter. Linda arrived at the park first and parked where Ewing had told her to park. She glanced at the cold bright sky, holding a red plaid blanket close to her, and began walking toward the park, a lonely, determined figure on this chilled winter afternoon. Ewing parked his car, spotted her, and walked toward her. Each feigned an air of not having the slightest idea of who the other was. This sham continued until they entered the park grounds together.

Deeper into the woods they went, passing tilted, rusted carcasses of several old Volkswagens and the stained hulks of abandoned refrigerators, tipped on their sides, with doors gone, and old egg stains still visible. They seemed to be looking for a lyrical place to billow the blanket down, a place of imagined moss and warm, kind sunlight. There was nothing like that. No matter where they looked as they trudged through the cold, tangled undergrowth—pine trees towering above, vines grabbing at their ankles - there just didn't seem to be an appropriate place to fornicate in private. This overgrown place had an aura of decay—not a fitting location for a romantic encounter between a prominent gynecologist and his patient, a respectable housewife and mother of two.

Finally, they spotted a little hollow, a cradle in the cold ground, and together, like young lovers, they took corners of the blanket and billowed it out. The blanket—that blanket that Linda and the children and I used to take on picnics and cookouts—seemed to settle reluctantly on the slightly wet undergrowth, on the unfriendly December ground. The two sat down on it tentatively as if, like a magic carpet, it might find this whole deal not to its liking and simply rise up, take flight, and go back to Pinckney Avenue where its conscience said it belonged.

Almost immediately Jim Ewing was wrestling his pants down to his chubby little ankles. His overcoat still on, he was positioning himself on top of my wife like some sort of urgent little bulldog who would not be denied.

There were no flowers in bloom at this time of the year, no winter birds, not even a stillness that might stir one's heart. The only semblance of light out of the ordinary was a muted reflection off that rusted VW bumper. With the option of choosing a warm, empty house with big beds, a roaring fire and zero risk, these two mature adults chose a blanket on the cold, damp winter ground in a public space. It didn't make sense - unless they were seeking the added element of risk for a heightened quality of arousal, buildup, and final climax. Ewing went at it like some sort of mud sloth, winter no deterrent, as if that was all God had programmed him to do. He simply went at it. My wife just happened to be what was under him.

"All right! What the hell are you two guys doing in there? Come out of there!" yelled a male voice in black uniform. The voice belonged to Officer Richard Gould of the Florence Police Department, and with those words, he completely botched a carefully choreographed scenario that Jan Warner and the detectives had devised. In hopes of catching the couple in the process of copulating in a public park, the police were supposed to have arrived precisely at the detectives' cue, but that got screwed up (pardon the pun). Instead, they were several minutes late to the party and their opportunity to maximize the advantage was lost. Meanwhile, the detectives observing from a distance of fifty or sixty feet were taking photographs, some including children in the background.

The two were up instantly gathering their belongings. "Where did you get that badge?" Ewing shouted at Gould. "At the Five and Dime?" In the list of dumb things to say to a cop, this one was at the top. The agents kept snapping photographs as the two lovebirds, walking briskly, tried to put the woods behind them, seeking their cars as quickly as they could. They had no idea how much of this had been filmed, including their shocked expressions, huddled postures, and Ewing trying to pretend it hadn't happened at all. They sped off from the park to their separate destinations without so much as a backward glance at each other.

En route home from Columbia, the children were exhausted and fell asleep in the car. While they slept, I stopped and telephoned Charles Ray. He updated me on what had occurred several hours before in the park. When we got home, it was close to 10:00 p.m. Linda had been home for hours following her eventful outing at the park. She and I had what may have been our final agreement as husband and wife: we agreed it would be best to put the children to bed fully clothed, as they were. I concentrated on bringing in stuff from the car - their toys, books, two small pillows, two blankets and their water bottles.

There was an incredibly loud silence between Linda and myself. I was sure she was puzzled about what I might have known about her little tryst in the woods because the two of them seemed to be beginning to put two and two together. The possibility of her saying anything at all to me was just hanging there so ripe for argument, but I wasn't about to reveal anything I knew yet.

After she put the children's things away that I'd brought in, she simply announced, "I'm going to bed." This incident, as bad as it seemed to be, in my mind, gave me more hope than I'd had to date. In a short while, I was in my room, and I turned on the recorder.

Linda: "Hello."
Ewing: "Hello."
Linda: "Did you call the police station yet?"
Ewing: "Yeah."
Linda: "What did they say?"

Ewing: "They said Gould is for real. He's the real thing. A cop. They didn't know anything about the other two guys."
Linda: "I wonder if private eyes ever work with the police?"
Ewing: "The two other guys were the ones taking the pictures. Maybe they were working with the police. Seems like an awful big coincidence to me, all of them there at once. Yeah, that was something like you'd see on TV."
Linda: "Wait until my in-laws see the pictures."

She was amused, cocky, arrogant, and exhibited no shame at all.

Ewing: "They wouldn't show that much anyhow."
Linda: "They were at the wrong angle, I hope. I don't know."
Ewing: "You just couldn't stay away. You just had to have it."
Linda: "Blame it on me."
Ewing: "Are you still going to see me in the morning?"
Linda: "Yeah, I will. And I'll wave from your balcony if they take more pictures."

She was so defiant and insensitive now that she was finding her escapades amusing; and her attitude had become unconscionable. This was not the woman I had married!

Ewing: "Well, you know if they're out to get you, they're going to get you. Maybe they were just bird watching."
Linda: "God, Jimmy!"
Ewing: "What a way to make a living!"
Linda: "Boy! Spying on people."
Ewing: "Of course, he could have your phone bugged too. You had made your mind up to tell him anyhow if he confronted you again, hadn't you?"

Linda: "I just hope they can't use the pictures against us. You know, in taking the children away from me. I don't think they can. But I don't know, he really loves those kids."

Ewing: "Enough to turn them away from their mother? It would be one thing if he could prove that you were running around every night with a different guy and that sort of thing. Neglecting the kids."

Linda: "That's true."

They didn't *think being a perverted sex addict would be an issue in a child custody matter*, I thought.

Ewing: "If they took the kids away from you, you would have visitation rights. Maybe taking them from you would be good. Would be for me."

Linda: "I don't know."

Ewing: "Would you stay with him for the kids?"

Linda: "I'd fight him first."

Ewing: "If you lose, what would you do?"

Linda: "I don't know. It would be a hard decision. I would really be torn between you and them."

That was an ominous statement, as the day might come when she would have to make that dreadful decision. For me, I thought, *the inability to love one's children, alone, is a non-negotiable flaw in one's character.* Knowing how he felt about his children in the very beginning should have been a disqualifier for her; but then, too, she was willing to put her children up for grabs. They had become birds of a feather!

Ewing: "I'm sure you'd make the right decision. Well, he's not going to know anything tonight."

Linda: "Yes, that's true. It's embarrassing, you know, to have pictures of it."

Ewing: "And my hair wasn't combed!... I don't feel like we've done anything wrong."

Apparently, neither one of these individuals thought they were doing anything wrong. They both suffered from a complete absence of conscience; so focused on their own individual interests that they were deceiving even themselves. Their arrogance was glaring. At this point, it was my hope they would continue this brash, reckless, irresponsible behavior to their undoing.

As for Linda, there was no hint of sorrow, concern, or reservations about the direction in which she was headed. There was only stoic determination to proceed, to get what she wanted, and I and the children would be dragged along behind her to her goal with no choice in the matter—except the one I had already made and had in progress, of which she was unaware. She had made her choice, leaving me no options. I was determined to move forward with matters as I knew to be in the best interest of our children.

She'd had plenty of warnings, plenty of offramps, plenty of opportunity to do the right thing or to prepare for what was to come, had she not been so preoccupied; so consumed by her compulsive drive for instinctual gratification. She knew on some level, that without her in my life, the children were my world. That had been made perfectly clear.

Linda: "He feels like he's losing his children. I don't know whether he'll try to fight me for them or not. They're usually awarded, I know, to the mother. But I'm ready to move on with this. He can visit the children. It was really nice to see you this afternoon."

CHAPTER ELEVEN

It was Saturday, December 30th. The pressure of holding inside all I knew was going on while continuing to interact with Linda seemed insurmountable. I was wearing down and with my lawyer, Jan Warner, who had become indescribably more important and closer than the typical hired legal aid, I had to be transparent. In a telephone conversation with Jan that morning, I expressed my doubt that I could continue this charade any longer without exploding.

"Not necessary," he said. "We have what we need. We're going to serve papers on her on Tuesday." That would be January 2, 1979, the day after New Year's.

Jan's announcement completely surprised me. It was the moment I had anxiously awaited; a moment like I had never experienced and will never forget. Mentally, I had kept my expectations low, but this gave me the burst of energy I sorely needed to boost myself for the days to follow. I had thought it would take more time than just twenty-five days to collect all the evidence needed to give my team the advantage we sought. But Linda and Ewing had been so persistent in their deeds, so egregious in their actions and so careless in their escapades, that no more evidence was needed. I felt I had held my breath almost an entire month, during which time I was almost constantly nauseated. I had thrown up numerous times and struggled with bouts of diarrhea. I had no appetite and had lost over thirty pounds. Soon I would no longer have to keep all this within me, although I needed to remain silent through New Year's Eve and New Year's Day about what was to occur on January 2nd, which was three days away. *Could I make it?*

Jan told me that as the party initiating the action (the complainant), we were to prepare all the documentation including the temporary custody order; and that he would "load up on her." He was confident the judge would sign the documents he put before him. I presumed the same would be the case for the action against Ewing, but I had little interest in that. At that moment, I knew that what I had waited for, at least preliminarily, was a foregone conclusion: I would be awarded temporary custody of the children. I knew that, into the future, it would take an extraordinary change in the circumstances to warrant any change in custody. The party with custody would have the advantage going forward. Jan was writing it up that way. The party without custody henceforth, would have to prove more favorable circumstances to the children to justify a change. It was an exhilarating moment for me, a peak point in my life. Inwardly, I was sky high!

In addition, Ewing would also be served on Tuesday with an alienation of affections lawsuit. Additional charges would be filed in that same complaint, including charges of criminal conversation (old English law for intimacy with the spouse of another) and malpractice. This degenerate who, it was later revealed, wantonly, indiscriminately preyed upon trusting and vulnerable women, this deviant sex predator who had brought horror upon my family and my life, Dr. James Ewing, was about to get his just due.

And Linda? All those years, days, and nights, like a cherished pearl necklace beaded slowly over time, a stream of time God had given us to go from couple to family with a wealth of promise ahead, had come to an end. Those pearls were all being spilled into a vat of warm, wet manure. Linda had aborted. She had done her damage, willed it specifically, flaunted it, had been cavalier about it and practically waved her infidelity in my face, making a mockery of our marriage and the vows we had taken almost eleven years before. She had lost all sense of decency and dignity. She was absorbed in herself every moment. The marriage had been ravaged and was over, and all with barely a thought for the impact on our children. It was not hard to feel how deserving she was of what was coming. She, too, was in line for a reckoning.

She hadn't expressed any doubt at all. No hesitation about her actions. Her rebellion had turned to confidence which had become arrogance that was somehow, in her mind, grounded in the legal system's automatic practice of awarding custody of children to the mother. Reflecting her arrogance, she was now actually finding her immoral and depraved actions comical. She assumed she would retain custody; but was willing to put that at risk for something that had become more important to her personally. She was willing to destroy anything in the path of her new goals and objectives. She let the fate of our family revolve around a man who, for a "romantic rendezvous," would take her into the cold, dank woods and lay her out with hulks of old cars and old nasty, rusting refrigerators for his afternoon pleasure. This was his idea. He may have been in control and orchestrating things, but she was far from blameless.

It was impossible to understand how she could come out to a temporary, tentative love as he was proposing, to an offer which seemed to have all the fine print and footnotes of a legal contract; as he had stated his willingness to commit to only 95 percent of his love to her - the other 5 percent to be reserved for his desire to be occasionally "seduced by another woman," because "I'm only human" and "it's an ego thing." In reality, he was the one doing the seducing. He was just full of it! Such a pattern of behavior for anyone, much less a doctor, is, in fact contemptible, considering the brief, shallow advantage it provides. Anyone who would find this philosophy at all acceptable is exceedingly naïve. And she was! Obsessed with maximizing the possibilities for his physical gratification, Ewing's chosen profession and area of specialty provided the ideal opportunity. His exhibited transgressions compressed over a few weeks with Linda would ultimately prove to be only one of many of his exploits with others to come to light. Obsessed by the impulse to seek more excitement for himself, the insatiable pervert was oblivious to what the more would cost everyone else. As for Linda, Louise Ewing had been one of her closest friends. Shortly, that would change. Their friendship was limited to only days.

Dr. Schnackenberg would testify to his psychiatric evaluations of the children, of me, and of my parents, who would be named as "intermediaries" for the children. He would suggest to the court that she seek psychiatric care because of her mental state that had been affected by her actions and inactions, and it was his opinion that she was not presently competent to parent the children, having locked David in his room and striking him on occasions. He would suggest she needed treatment and counseling.

The detectives would testify about every incident that had occurred. They hadn't missed a beat! They would provide photographs documenting and validating their surveillance of each of the incidences that had occurred. Photographs of the two in McLeod Park with children on their bicycles in the background. Photos of our children left alone outside the house while Linda was on the phone with Ewing for extended periods. Photos of her entering and leaving his office building at times when his offices were officially closed. Photos of Ewing entering and then departing our home at night in my absence.

To get away from her after breakfast that next morning, Saturday, December 30th, and, perhaps to give her a little more rope to hang herself, if that were needed, I dressed the children early and took them with me to my office and then to make rounds at various construction sites.

Was there any doubt in my mind that she would immediately leave the house and go and meet with Ewing? None. It was no longer a fair guessing contest: the behavior had become predictable. The children and I came back home around eleven o'clock. She wasn't home. While David and Jade played downstairs in their playroom, I quickly checked the recorder. I pressed the PLAY button, and my suspicions were validated. I could only assume they had forgotten their suspicion that "he could have your phone bugged too." But then, I attributed their determination to proceed to their defiance and arrogance.

Linda: "Did you see any white cars around?"

I didn't know what the detectives were driving, but I assumed from this comment that the detectives were driving white cars.

Ewing: "Where are you?"
Linda: "Home. They've left. So, I can come and see you if you want?"
Ewing: "Yeah, come on."

At about 1:00 p.m. she returned home. The children and I were sitting at the kitchen table having our lunch. As though we were undeserving of an excuse, she gave no indication of where she had been and did not join us at the table. I presumed excuses were no longer necessary; as she would soon be booting me out and not having to deal with me anyway. After the children's naps, I drove them to our most visited spot, the church playground, and afterward, I called Charles Ray from a nearby phone booth to see what, if anything, they had on Linda's whereabouts a few hours earlier.

They had gotten them again. He read to me from notes:

"Agent set up surveillance at the Baumrind residence at 10:15 a.m. Agent observed Mrs. Baumrind's blue Buick station wagon leave the driveway and agent followed her. Mrs. Baumrind drove downtown and parked her car behind the hospital. Agent cut the block and observed Mrs. Baumrind walking across the street to the Medical Center Building. Agent identified Dr. Ewing's blue MG parked behind the Medical Center Building. Agent followed Mrs. Baumrind into the building and observed her as she entered the rear door of Dr. Ewing's office. No one else was seen entering the office. Agent knocked on the front door several times, but no one came to the door. Agent knocked on the rear door twice, but no one would answer. At 12:15 Mrs. Baumrind came out of the rear door of Dr. Ewing's office. She was wearing blue slacks with a beige sweater and carrying a tan pocketbook. At 12:17, Dr. Ewing exited his side office entrance and walked directly to his car in the parking lot. Agent discontinued surveillance."

Now there was no question about her thinking only of herself. After the incident in the park, less than twenty-four hours earlier, surely she knew her children were more at stake than ever—or she should have. Regardless, she continued her behavior as though nothing else was as important to her as this torrid relationship of hers. Totally insensitive to who she may be hurting and the trauma that would be caused, her actions were blatant and reckless. Her brain had pivoted from obsession to compulsion. Was she now devoured by addiction herself, like Ewing?

We got back from the park at around 4 p.m. and I took the children into our backyard to the swings. Back and forth, back and forth they swung. It had been 25 days since my enlightening in this very spot. 25 days of my life swinging back and forth, back and forth between desperation and hope. As I pushed them up to the sky, my chest filled with a terrible choking sadness - not for all the tapes I'd listened to or the knowledge of their secret rendezvous or because of the tomb-like silence now in our house. It was because of the fact that, obviously, Linda didn't care. I knew I was inconsequential. But shockingly, it seemed to me the children didn't fare much better as runners-up to him. Her heart was somewhere else. For the thrills and excitement this sleazy, festering, insufferable pervert who, along with society, called himself a doctor offered her, she had abandoned her family.

It was a habit now that I detested; but that night the tape recordings rendered more evidence, though probably not needed. Was there any chance at all that I would hear her tell Ewing this was all a terrible mistake? That she had had a good husband? That this all had to end? Those thoughts were quickly dashed, and the reality of the situation crystallized with this sobering conversation.

Ewing: "Well, we almost had a nice afternoon in the park, didn't we? Did you enjoy it?"

Linda: "Yeah, tomorrow will be better."
Ewing: "I've got to get you to relax again."
Linda: "My throat's kind of scratchy."
Ewing: "I can give you something for that." [both cynics laugh] "You really went after it this morning, didn't you?"

Linda laughed again. I didn't find this funny. Then the conversation turned to orgasms.

Ewing: "You've got me curious now. What's the difference? What's the difference between a big orgasm and a little one?"

The man's a gynecologist, I thought. He knows the answer very well to this basic question. I was hoping she would say to him, "Now, Jimmy, you know very well the answer to that question. You're just fishing for a direct response from me for the sick thrill of hearing it from me personally. It's a turn on to you. You're nothing but a pervert! Now get the hell out of my life!" But instead, disappointingly, she responded,

Linda: "Sometimes, the big ones are so big that you can't stand them. I become so sensitive that I can't stand it."
Ewing: "But you're going to live with it, right?" [He laughs.] "Have you had many big ones or are most of them little ones?"

He asked as though he was a scientist in a laboratory posing necessary questions, testing hypotheses to formulate theory; but more like a sick pervert salivating to hear her detailed response.

Linda: "Don't you remember a big one a couple of weeks ago? Remember?"
Ewing: "No."
Linda: "You don't remember it? Well. Let's not talk about it."
Ewing: "Have you ever had a big one with Vernon?"
Linda: "Not in a long time. More early in the marriage."
Ewing: "Have you ever given yourself a big one?"
Linda: "It's almost impossible to give myself a small one, let alone a big one."

Ewing droned on with his unquenchable quest for more salacious details.

Ewing: "You told me the other night you just zipped one off in a hurry."
Linda: "That must have been Wednesday when you had to call off our meeting."

What! I thought. *So, had she, herself, become an addict like him? That quick? Requiring a daily fix? Whether with or without him?*

Ewing: "Yeah, I guess so."
Ewing: "Did he ask you where you were?"
Linda: "No. Boy, this week is going to be bad."
Ewing: "When do you think you'll have the big pow-wow?"
Linda: "I wonder if he'll say, 'go ahead, leave, but the children stay.' I wonder if I can just pack them up and take them?"
Ewing: "I don't know about divorces."
Linda: "I don't either."

I didn't know either, I thought, but I had a giant of a lawyer who did know. In the unavoidable clash ahead, my giant might just consume this sex pervert monster parading as a doctor.

Ewing: "Looks like the only thing you could pin on him would be mental cruelty or something like that."
Linda: "Yeah. Boy, that's a hard one. That's what everybody claims, though."

Finally, here was some recognition that she had little to no justification for dumping her husband for this new and exciting doctor. After all the love she had been given all these years, at least, I felt somewhat vindicated that the only thing she could pin on me was "mental cruelty." Ultimately, there was never any attempt to follow up on that suggestion, however. They must have determined that this fabricated charge could not be substantiated. Still, I could not shake the thought that surely there was something I could have done differently for her to have loved me and not left me.

Ewing: "Yes, of course, he could go for adultery on you."
Linda: "Yeah. He can prove it now."
Ewing: "Yeah, got pictures of us screwing! …Has he gone to bed?"
Linda: "No, he's upstairs. This whole thing's really getting me upset now."
Ewing: "Yeah, it's exciting, like on TV. Maybe we can sell pictures to some magazine, or maybe you'll get your picture in the newspaper. Bunch of trouble! I mean brushes with the law, the underground. I don't know why I put up with it."

This man's arrogance was over the top. And society held him in high regard! I was hoping the adage was true that "the higher they rise, the greater they fall."

Linda: "I don't know either, except maybe that you like me a little bit. Yeah, one minute to the next, you don't know whether I'm going to be crying or laughing or sane or insane."

I likened this conversation of theirs to two addicts who seek to mitigate stress and don't choose a healthy solution. Instead, they run from the pain of reality to the pleasure of momentary euphoria. It had become very clear by now that Linda had no inner compass and, seemingly, no conscience; or she was ignoring what conscience she did have. I had no power to do anything about what was happening. It was very sad to see this happening; knowing that ignoring one's conscience has its consequences.

CHAPTER TWELVE

Sunday, December 31, 1978, was a blur. The next day was Monday, January 1, 1979. Happy New Year? My turbulent mix of emotions did not include "happy," only relief and perhaps anticipation that some big things were about to happen that could help me and the children. The following day, Linda and Ewing would be served. Knowing this, when Linda was busy in the kitchen preparing for lunch, I went into her bedroom and removed her credit cards that were in my name. I also took envelopes containing money for the children from family members from her dresser drawer. I had already closed out our joint checking account, the children's savings accounts and would soon deposit the children's money in new accounts out of Linda's reach. As well, I had changed the beneficiaries on my life insurance policies.

Jade had been put down for a nap. I told Linda that I was taking David with me to the office to change air filters. I put the child in his car seat, got in the driver's seat myself and put the key in the ignition. I turned the key, starting the engine, then, hesitated several moments. I switched the ignition off. I realized the moment had arrived. Armed with the knowledge now that papers would be served the next day, and now with absolutely nothing to lose legally by doing so, I felt an uncontrollable compulsion to confront Linda. I'd tolerated all I was going to take without her knowing I'd been aware of exactly what had been going on. I turned my head and told David to stay in his seat in the car, that I was going back into the house and would be back in a few minutes. I exited the car and went quickly into the house where Linda had gone into the den. I strode up into her face and the bottled-up pressure of emotions of months of abuse from her came spewing out of me unbridled.

"Linda, if I ever come home again and find that son of a bitch pervert in my house or on my property, I'll kill him with my bare hands. The two of you think you're so clever. Screwing him in our home with our children present, at his office, in the park and elsewhere! Watching pornographic movies with him. You have no sense of decency! It's all documented - everything you've been doing with that bastard. You're a deceitful, irresponsible slut! You don't even resemble the woman I married. I don't recognize anything about you that made me love you. You've demeaned and degraded me. And our children? You haven't given them any consideration in your thoughts and actions. I'll see you in court and, yes - you've been wondering for several weeks now - I'll be asking for a divorce on grounds of adultery and for custody of our children." I said nothing about the wiretap or what was in store for Ewing. I had just delivered in two minutes what her conscience had not in months of time to do so.

The tears came immediately, flowing down her face and she collapsed to my legs, grabbing onto me, and pleading with me not to divorce her. I reminded her how hard I had tried with her, the many attempts I had made, all to no avail—for months. She continued to plead with me not to divorce her and not to take the children away from her. The abrupt change of heart was not convincing. I wasn't going to fall for this, remembering their many recorded words, including these:

Ewing: "Would you stay with him for the kids?"
Linda: "I'd fight him first."
Ewing: "If you lose, what would you do?"
Linda: "It would be a hard decision. I would really be torn between you and them."

    I told her she would be served with papers Tuesday and pulled her to her feet and said, "It's too late! You're a fraud. I have zero faith in what you tell me. Deceit is all you know!" Inwardly, I was torn up too - torn with feelings of wanting to save our family and marriage but knowing now that in reality it really wasn't possible and would never be. She didn't have the capacity to be genuine, and no one knew that better than I did. I would never be able to trust her again. The fact was; however, I had been equally as deceptive for a month in concealing what I knew was going on and in gathering evidence. I had taken the offense and had been as determined and as consistent in my behavior as they had been in theirs.

    By this time, David had come into the den. He had found a way to extricate himself from the car seat. I must not have buckled him in properly, and my tirade had taken longer than I had anticipated. And little Jade was crying in her room, having awakened from her nap, perhaps as a result of the commotion in the den which was connected to her bedroom where she'd slept as her mother and the doctor had copulated on the carpet in front of the roaring fireplace a week or so before. David and I went into Jade's room and dressed her. I took the children from the house to the car, put them in their car seats, and we drove to the nearby park.

DECEIT

    Allowing the children to play by themselves, I sat there thinking. I knew how traumatic my outburst had been for her. It was traumatic for me! I empathized with her, but the eruption had been both exhilarating and cathartic for me. I found myself wondering whether I'd done the right thing. Hadn't we had many good times together? And the children - they were hers and mine together. I wanted to share them with her. I didn't want to deprive her of them, or them of her. But I was not going to allow her to deprive me of them either. I was left with no choice. I felt, and will always be grateful, for these precious children that she had birthed. The happy memories of the good times and all we had shared were smothered in my mind by the agony, the terrible pain of hers and his recorded voices, and the knowing of all that had taken place between the two of them, including Ewing's lurid post-coital details, and her plans to supplant me in her life and in the lives of our children. I knew she didn't have it in her heart to feel any of this, as I did, and, so, I knew I had to proceed with matters as they were.

    I would learn from Charles Ray that as soon as the children and I had left the house, Linda exited the house, drove directly to Ewing's house, and they drove away in separate cars. The wiretap was still intact. Later, it would reveal that as soon as I had left with the children, she called Ewing and told him, "He knows everything! He's had us under surveillance. He's going to serve papers on me for divorce and custody of the children. He knows all kinds of things. He knows you've been showing me pornographic movies. How could that be?" Ewing: "Then he's got you bugged! We can't talk."

    They agreed she would immediately drive down to his house and they'd go off somewhere private to talk.

That would be the final night Linda and I remained together in the house, but separately in our individual rooms—I, in my bedroom upstairs, David in the room next to me, and Jade in her room downstairs next to Linda in the master bedroom.

The night of confrontation I went to bed around midnight. *At* 4:30 a.m. I awoke in a daze sensing someone standing over me. It was Linda. The light from the street cast a haze and her silhouette was framed against the window. As I swung my legs out of bed and stood up beside her in the dark, still dazed, she said, "Vernon, we've had a good life together. It was just a romantic thing. Couldn't we try again?"

Her words floated in my head, ringing artificial. They were words I had longed to hear, but they were coming too late and fell far short of what needed to be said. Start over? Just like that? I had been trying for months, essentially begging her. It had been humiliating. Had she forgotten my persistent efforts to retrieve her love without any sustaining response from her? Was I supposed to simply dismiss all her insensitive remarks, and her brazen, belligerent behavior? Forgive her preoccupation with cheating and lying, and her deceitful actions? Forget about her unwillingness to take any action toward reconciling, to admit categorically that her actions had been wrong. Instead, all she could offer was a feeble excuse for her actions: "It was just a romantic thing." She expected me to let my defenses down and to take the risks she rightly should be assuming, even if she had been sincere, when I had for months just been an obstacle in her way to Dr. Ewing. A Quid Pro Quo arrangement could only work if there was trust, but I was the only trustworthy one between us.

DECEIT

For months and even this night, confronted by my recognition of her behavior and actions, she wouldn't admit how wrong she had been. She hadn't said this was all a terrible mistake, that she wanted her family back, that she would get Ewing out of her life. She expressed no sorrow, no remorse, offered no apologies, and had not asked for forgiveness. She hadn't said any of the things I knew I would be saying to express my sincerity had I been her. As much as I wished in my heart that I could take her in my arms, love her and make all the bad go away, I knew her change of heart was not genuine and I was not going to risk what I had gained to help her change her circumstances. I knew her response had been prompted solely by her plight in being found out. I wasn't risking the children!

So much had happened. She had become a different person. She had invited this man into her life; being more involved with him than with our own children. She shouldn't have to be told what she should say or do, and she, herself, just didn't have it in her heart and conscience to do the right thing, had she been sincere. She hadn't been any better at acting than I was - actually worse! I kept thinking of how she had intended to oust me, but still allow me to babysit for her on weekends, until she told him, I "would probably grow tired of that and would eventually stop coming for the children so often." After all this time, all these years of living together, she didn't know me very well at all, enough to know the lengths to which I would go for my children! But then, maybe she didn't love the children as much as I did. There was no "maybe" about it. I knew she didn't love them like I did. This had just been demonstrated. But then, maybe I didn't know her very well either. Perhaps I was the one with the head in the clouds? Perhaps I had not recognized her lack of character, her capacity to do the things she had done. Or perhaps I had realized there were flaws, but had been in denial and was deceiving myself? Perhaps all of the above was true. We both had new things to learn about each other that had been overlooked in the past.

After asking me, "Couldn't we try again," she begged me to make love to her. Hard as that was to turn down, I wasn't exchanging that for my children and jeopardizing my case for custody, as she had done. All I could think of was the solid month, and likely longer, of incessant lovemaking she had just had with Ewing. Jan Warner had warned me against cohabitating with her in any way. Doing so would be viewed by the court as my having absolved her of all that had happened previously. It would be perceived as my having accepted her behavior and having forgiven her; and that acceptance on my part would negate all that had been accomplished to date. He repeated his advice that her adulterous behavior did not automatically constitute cause for the court to take children away from a mother, that judges could be capricious—that it is never known how a judge will respond to testimony until the decision is pronounced. I wasn't going to forfeit the children with one rash act. I insisted that she go back downstairs to her room. Once she was gone, I dismantled the recording device, removed the wires extending to the junction box near ground level at the rear of the house, and then, packed away the extension phone and devices that had facilitated the wiretap. We still did not know whether the wiretap would be ruled legal or not, and it would be best if the device and evidence of the tap were not discovered in my absence from the home. The wiretap had served its purpose.

Turning her away was the saddest moment of my life; one I will never forget, a moment that is seared into my soul. Actually, I'll never forget any of those moments in December 1978—all bad, several months of very bad memories. Hellacious memoirs they are! I wished that it was possible to wave a magic wand and make everything just a terrible nightmare so that we could take a deep breath, hold our family tight and go off happily into the future together, but it was not possible; and would never be. Her true self was now too well displayed. What would have prevented her from deceiving me again in the future, and reconnecting with him? It all boiled down to that thought—and I knew the answer. There was zero trust! Zero confidence in anything she could say. Too much water had passed under the bridge.

It was very, very painful, but I had turned her away. I had condemned my own family forever, for good or bad! They were terrible moments in that bleak month of December 1978, but this exchange with Linda contained the most dreadful moments of my life.

CHAPTER THIRTEEN

The next morning, Tuesday January 2nd, 1979, Jan Warner called me to advise that he would be in Florence by 11:00 a.m. to file the order in the divorce-custody matter and the complaint against Ewing, and he would see me in my office around 1:00 p.m. He arrived a few minutes late, stating that the judge had awarded me temporary custody until formal hearings could be held within approximately ninety days at which time the divorce and final custody would be granted. He warned me to be aware that custody is never permanent. Either party can institute custody proceedings if it can be established that circumstances have changed materially affecting the welfare of the children. His words would ring true for me: in the years ahead, as there would be multiple attempts by Linda to reverse and regain custody. However, based on the children's continuing stable, healthy circumstances, custody would not be changed.

Jan asked to make copies of these documents on my office copy machine to distribute and to be served on both Linda and Ewing. They had been executed by the family court judge and the Clerk of Court and recorded. He made the copies and put them down in front of me for my signature.

I prayed to God I was doing the right thing because I knew there was no turning back. The efforts of opposing attorneys and the indifferent mechanics of the legal process were underway now. Bad circumstances were about to be made much worse. I was given one copy of each set of the papers: one to Linda, the other to Ewing. Jan Warner kept one set and handed the others to Charles Ray, the detective, who had arrived shortly before. Charles was there as the official process server. I had not told Linda that Ewing would be served. Jan did not want to alert him.

Right after Jan Warner's earlier telephone call that morning, Linda called me, begging me to come home, imploring me to "think of us." She was distraught. She'd had a tearful and frightening morning, she told me, not knowing what to expect or when it would happen; but knowing full well her former world was about to crash down on her that day. I told her I was sorry, but it was too late for that, and I said goodbye. I felt her pain, but I had to leave it with her. I couldn't provide her the comfort an adoring husband would. I always had, but not this time. By taking legal action as I had, I was the cause of the discomfort. This did not make me feel good, but my actions had been preceded by and in direct response to her irresponsible behavior. The children were home with her. I worried about them, in her distress, but knew I'd be with them in a few hours.

Jan Warner departed for Sumter, and I drove home with Charles Ray who was following me in his car - yes, the white one - with the documents to be served on Linda and Ewing. It was a beautiful winter day with a clear, brilliant sky. As instructed by Jan, Charles went to the front door of our home and rang the doorbell, and when Linda answered, he handed her the papers advising her that she had been served. She was given five minutes to read the "order," at which time Charles called me to come into the house to get the children.

Charles remained in the house to assure that all went without incident. I was to pack up their belongings for three days and to take the children to my parents' home in Marion, twenty-five miles away. Linda was given three days to vacate the house. I felt this whole process was cruel; but that's exactly what she had been to me for months.

Charles went down the street to serve Ewing. As it turned out, Ewing was not home. His wife was served instead. Months later, Louise expressed her anger at me for her having been "served with Jimmy's papers." She told me that was how she'd learned of the explicit details of what had been occurring between Jimmy and Linda, her "best friend." I'm not sure she ever forgave me for that "brutal offense" of mine, but the manner of the summons delivery was not something over which I had any control. Like me, she was an innocent victim who was emotionally brutalized and had her life turned upside down by the same illicit relationship that had been thrust upon both of us.

When I walked into our house, Linda was sobbing, sitting in the living room with the papers in her lap. She looked up at me and asked through her tears "What are you going to do to me, Vernon?"

I felt three feet high and like the saddest excuse for a loving husband. The court "order" she had read already provided the details of what was to occur. I responded that I was following instructions in the judge's order and that I was taking the children. She was totally cooperative - submissive, pitiful. In silence, tearfully, room to room, side by side, she helped me gather the children's things, taking clothes out of drawers and putting them in a suitcase. David and Jade and I left the house with her home alone. The anger that I had felt about the circumstances for weeks had melted away to sorrow for us, for the children and for her as well.

DECEIT

The order outlined her flagrant adulterous relationship with Ewing (actually, it specified an unnamed man "well-known to the respondent") and asked for custody of the minor children and an immediate hearing in four days. She was given a mere four days to find an attorney and to prepare and present her case. Jan Warner knew all the angles to disadvantage his opponent. She would have to appear in family court on January 5th at which time she would have to show cause as to why the children should not be put in the temporary custody of the petitioner. It further required that she show why she should not have to undergo psychiatric evaluation and assist in the therapy of the children. It gave her permission to visit the children at specified times with the explicit warning that she should not try to remove them from the jurisdiction of the court.

The petition in the "order to show cause" stated three causes of action against her. The first accused her of having sex with Ewing while being married to the petitioner, and that she had engaged in these acts in her home and other places. It accused her of not only participating in sexual intercourse with the paramour but having 'unnatural sex', including these activities in public places, where the general public, including small children, were exposed to these illicit activities. Further, it specified that she had refused to continue marriage counseling that may have been helpful to the family, and that her attitude toward the petitioner and the children had become insensitive and calloused. The "first cause of action" asked for a complete and final divorce on the grounds of adultery.

The second cause of action claimed she was irresponsible as a mother and a wife; that she had neglected the children while involved with Ewing, that she was unstable in her behavior and further that she had lost interest in the children, spending little time with them, allowing them to roam around unsupervised and that I, the petitioner, had become a surrogate mother over the past months. She was not to interfere with the psychiatric needs of the children.

The third cause of action stated that because of her adulterous relationship with Ewing she was not entitled to alimony, support, or maintenance. I was to purchase her equity in the marital home at market value, and I and the children would resume our lives there in the home three days from January 2nd. She was to get no attorney fees or any relief from the cost of litigation resulting from her adulterous conduct. She was required to move out of the house, and I was to give her sufficient funds to secure a place to live.

The complaint served on Ewing also stated three causes of action. The first cause of action stated his address and profession of obstetrics and gynecology. It noted that Linda was my wife and had been since December 1967 and that we had two children from the marriage, ages five and two-and-a-half. The essence of the complaint was that at different times and places, and up to that date, the plaintiff had been deprived of his wife's protection, society, aid, and support, that Ewing had willfully, maliciously, intentionally, wrongfully, and unjustifiably gained the affection of Linda and enticed her from me. She had fallen for his tactics as a result of his deliberate and malicious actions.

He had caused the marriage to deteriorate, and he was encouraging her to leave the plaintiff. He had enticed her to spend time with him at different places over several months, and he promised her sexual pleasures during these times together. He had managed to get her to leave her home to meet him, resulting in the neglect of her own family. The

DECEIT

first action requested actual and punitive damages in the amount of $275,000.

The second cause of action against Ewing related to the plaintiff's loss of pride, public image, reputation, and other aspects associated with the role of a father, husband, and businessman. Disgraced and humiliated, the court was asked to award the Plaintiff $325,000.

The third cause of action, the misuse of his medical knowledge and access to private and personal information used to seduce Linda was a breach of medical ethics that had resulted in the destruction of the Baumrind family for which the court was asked to award the plaintiff $250,000.

I would not have traded $850,000 or any other amount of money for the wife, family, and life I had prior to all of this. At the initial divorce-custody hearing in family court chambers on January 5th the judge heard the arguments. Linda had secured an attorney to represent her. On January 10th, the judge issued his written order. This order granted temporary custody of David and Jade to me and reasonable visitation rights to Linda, as follows:

1. Linda would have the children on the first and third weekend of each month from 6:00 p.m. on Sunday until 12:00 noon on Tuesday.
2. She would have visitation on the second and fourth weeks of each month from Tuesday noon until 6:00 p.m. Wednesday.
3. She was to pick the children up at their home and return them at the proper times.
4. Linda would have to be responsible during the times the children were with her for their school, doctor, dentist, and any other activities.

5. She was restrained from removing the children from the state or trying to circumvent the order of the court in any way.
6. My parents were designated as intervenors to assist me with the care of the children for as long as needed.
7. The children were to continue for as long as necessary in therapy with Dr. Schnackenberg, and Linda was to cooperate with him.
8. The children and I were to live in the marital home and Linda was to move out. I was to help Linda move out of the house and find another place for her to live. She was allowed to remove sufficient items from the house necessary to set up a home for herself.
9. I was required to pay her $400 per month, give her an automobile, and maintain insurance on her car. I was to provide her with medical insurance.
10. It was suggested that Linda seek an independent psychiatric evaluation for herself, but she was to be responsible for the fees.
11. The court allowed us to seek marriage counseling if we desired to do so.

The children had known security in the comfort of a home with a mother and father, such as it was from the Fall of 1978 to the date of the hearing. Now they would be in a shuttled kind of existence, having to accept a visit with their mother and then a return to life with me, only to be broken again in a few days by another short visit with their mother. They were expected to turn their love on and off as the calendar dictated, and to develop normal emotional

DECEIT

personalities in the process. That was the challenge - to develop normal emotional personalities. Despite this challenge, my ultimate goal with the children was to raise them with exemplary qualities of character that would enable them to become responsible parents and productive citizens capable of avoiding a repeat of their mother's perverse behavior with similar consequences.

Two days later, on the 12th of January, Ewing's attorney, Robert Page, replied to the complaint served on his client, Dr. James Ewing. Their response follows:

1. He denied each and every allegation not hereinafter admitted, modified, or explained.
2. He alleged that he and the plaintiff and their families had been friends and neighbors for a number of years, and that plaintiff's marital relationship had deteriorated, caused by events and matters over which he had not been associated nor over which he had any control.

CHAPTER FOURTEEN

On February 6, 1979, in the matter of the lawsuit against Dr. Ewing, I sat face-to-face across a table in deposition with this man. We met in a simple hearing room, no judge present—just him and me, his attorney and mine, and a court transcriber.

As Jan began to question him, it was obvious that in matters dealing with sex he would simply either proclaim that he was counseling with Linda about her marital problems or he would take the Fifth Amendment, or his attorney, Robert Page, would assert those privileges for him.

Jan went over a list of visits Linda made to Ewing's office. This list had been provided in advance of the deposition in response to a request for such that had the power of subpoena behind it.

Jan questioned the doctor, "This would be the complete record of your treatments and you don't remember any other or calls that were made to you by this lady, or you to her, concerning problems that she had?"

"That's correct," said Ewing.

"Was anyone else in the office when you and she met to discuss these matters?" Jan asked.

"No," he responded.

"When did you first meet with her in your office?"

"October and November."

"How many times did you meet with her."

"I didn't keep a diary, but I'd say between four and six times."

"Do you remember when you met her in her home?"

"No, I don't. I think Mr. Baumrind knows that date."

"You say, Mr. Baumrind knows?"

"Yes"

"Have you discussed this with Mr. Baumrind?"

"No, but I understand now, he knew about everything in advance."

"Did you meet with her at any other places?"

"A couple of times," he responded.

"Did you ever enter her house by going down an alleyway behind her home, leading to the rear side of it?"

"Yes"

"What part of the house did you have these meetings in?" Jan asked.

"The den."

"Where were the Baumrind children?"

"They were both in bed,"

"Where were their beds, Dr. Ewing?"

"I believe one was sleeping upstairs and one was downstairs in another room."

"And the one child that was sleeping closest to the den - can you tell me about how far away that was from where you and Mrs. Baumrind were holding this meeting?"

"It was a connecting room I believe," Ewing said.

"What did you and Mrs. Baumrind do during the hour-and-a-half meeting that you had in the Baumrind home in late December when you were there?"

Mr. Page interjected, "We object. I'm instructing him not to answer that question on the grounds that it might tend to incriminate him. I don't know what his answer is, but that is how I am instructing him to respond."

"Doctor," Jan said, "let me put it this way. At this meeting in her den, did you and Mrs. Baumrind discuss her marital problems?"

"We discussed the issues she was having with her husband."

"Tell me, Dr. Ewing, are you a marriage counselor, as well as an obstetrician-gynecologist?"

"No, Sir."

"Dr. Ewing, tell me, sir, what went on at McLeod Park the afternoon of December thirtieth amongst the decayed refrigerators and the rusting vehicles?"

"Well, we went for a walk in the park and then we went to the back corner and got well off the beaten path and just sat down on a blanket."

"Did you discuss her marital problems in the park on that day?"

At that point, Mr. Page objected to the question: "We object. I'm instructing him not to answer the question on the grounds that it might incriminate him. I don't know what his answer is but that is how I am instructing him."

"Doctor, let me ask you this," Jan said, "This answer you filed, you had it sworn to before you signed it, didn't you?"

"Yes."

"Then you realize your verification of this answer makes the allegations thereof sworn to as true by you. Isn't that correct?"

"Right," said Ewing.

"Do you know what Mr. Baumrind has sued you for?

He responded, "Number One, alienation of affections of his wife."

"So, you did realize that didn't you?"

"Yes."

"And in your response, you deny under oath that you alienated the affections of his wife? Is that correct?"

Ewing and his attorney conferred with one another. Squirming against the light of the truth, Ewing responded, "I denied the charges as stated in the summons."

"All right. Then the second action was an action against you for what is commonly known as 'criminal conversation.' In other words, that you and his wife engaged sexual intercourse, which was outside of her marriage vows. And you denied, under oath, in your answer that you and she had engaged in sexual intercourse, did you not?"

"I denied the charges as they were stated in the summons,"

"Let me ask you this doctor. You knew that Mr. and Mrs. Baumrind were living together, didn't you?"

"Of course!"

"And you engaged in sexual intercourse with Mrs. Baumrind at your office, at your house, at her house, in the park?"

Mr. Page again recited the doctor's Fifth Amendment privileges.

Jan then asked Ewing, "Was your wife aware of the fact that you were talking to Mrs. Baumrind on a daily basis?"

"Well, of course," Ewing responded. "When we were going on the walks, she was aware of it because Linda was alone, but she didn't really know. She knew I called her a couple of times on the telephone but not on a daily basis."

"Doctor," said Jan, "did you tell Mrs. Baumrind how to get rid of her husband? How to get him out of the house?"

"No."

"Did you ever tell her that she should leave her husband?"

"I didn't initially. Now after she told me that she was planning to and that she didn't love him any longer, I tended to agree."

"Now getting back to the time that you showed her those X-rated movies in your house, I think I asked you whether or not you and she had sexual intercourse and you told me that you would not answer on the basis that it may tend to incriminate you. Is that correct?"

"That's correct."

"Let me ask you this. Didn't she tell you she had not seen an X-rated movie before?"

"Yes."

"Have you and she engaged in cunnilingus or fellatio during this period of time?"

Mr. Page asserted his Fifth Amendment rights.

"Did Mrs. Baumrind tell you that she had admitted to Mr. Baumrind the relationship that you and she were having?"

"Well, I think she did after we knew we were being followed but she didn't before."

"When did you know you were being followed?"

Well, the afternoon we saw the three men chasing down on us."

"That was the twenty-ninth of December?"

"I guess along about that date."

"And you and she had just been sitting on the blanket that day just discussing her marital problems?"

"Just sitting. Correct. We had been sitting on the blanket."

"You and she had not been committing any type of intercourse or sexual act?"

Mr. Page asserted his client's Fifth Amendment rights.

"Dr. Ewing, I'm asking you to take a look at these photographs taken in the park. On the twenty-ninth of December, in the park, were you and she partially or totally unclothed?"

"We object on the same grounds," asserted Mr. Page. "I instruct him not to answer."

"All right," Jan said, "have you and she been unclothed in each other's presence since October 1978?"

"Object on the same grounds," Page droned. "I instruct him not to answer."

I looked at Jan, and he glanced at me with a little sideways shake of his head; both of us recognizing the absurdity of the proceeding.

"Now, Dr. Ewing, is it correct or incorrect that about two and a half months before the first of January of 1979 that you would call Mrs. Baumrind most mornings at around ten o'clock?"

"No, not every morning," said Ewing.

"Would you call her about ten o'clock after you finished your hospital rounds and got to your office on most mornings between that period?"

"I called several times "Ewing said. "I wouldn't say almost every morning."

"Would she tell you that Mr. Baumrind was in the house while she was calling you?"

Ewing thought a moment, "She admitted to that, yes."

"Doctor, did you tell Mrs. Baumrind that if Mr. Baumrind was out of the house that you could see her more frequently?"

"No."

"At any time, did you discuss with Mrs. Baumrind the proper way to engage in fellatio?"

Mr. Page again cited the provisions of the Fifth Amendment.

"Doctor, can you tell me any reason you did not want Mr. Baumrind to know that you were talking to his wife?"

"I don't think he liked the idea of me talking to her."

"One final question, doctor, did you, at any time, advise Mrs. Baumrind to terminate her marriage with Mr. Baumrind?"

"Well, she was unhappy, and I tended to agree that it would be best."

"So, you tended to agree that this marriage would not work out?"

"Well, that wasn't evident the first of October, but it became evident as things progressed."

After Ewing's deposition was finished, I, in turn, was deposed by Robert Page beginning with basic facts of my life—age, college, marital status, number of children, profession, and so on. Then he proceeded with specifics.

"Mr. Baumrind, you are a businessman here in Florence, I believe, aren't you?"

"I am, sir."

"Are you in Real Estate?"

"I am."

"What is your age?"

"Thirty-four."

"Are you a college graduate?"

"I am."
"And you have two children?"
"Yes, a five-year-old son and a two-year-old daughter."
"Did Dr. Ewing deliver both children?"
"No Sir. He delivered just the two-year-old."
"Did your two families up until, let's say, October of this year - that seems to be about the time the problems began to surface - until that time did the families visit back and forth from time to time?"
"We visited several times."
"Did you have any hostilities toward Doctor Ewing and his wife?"
"No sir."
"Was there any particular reason on your part why you didn't join into the mutual activities of the two families?"
"Sir, if you are referring to the period October 1978 into December 1978, I think the only time I joined in was when the Ewings visited us briefly to see our Christmas tree. Otherwise, I didn't join in on the only other activity that I'm aware of - the occasional evening walks in the neighborhood - because we have two small children at home and one of us needed to stay with those children for their regular evening routines before bedtime. If you're referring to the period prior to October 1978, there were several times the Ewings and we went out dining and to a movie together, sometime before October 1978."
"All right," said Page. "This is of a personal nature, but are you aware of any sexual problems that you and your wife had?"
"I was never aware of any," I said,
"Not aware of any?" said Page,
"Not until these recent events," I said.

"Had you and your wife ever separated?"

"No, sir."

"When you started going to the marriage counselor with your wife, were you aware of any relationship between her and Dr. Ewing?"

"No, sir," I said.

"How did you first learn that there was such a relationship?"

"I suspected in early December."

"When did you become suspicious?" Page asked.

"Early December," I responded.

"Do you remember the date?"

"Sir, I believe it was December sixth."

"And how did you confirm your suspicions?"

"I was with my children that afternoon while my wife had said she would be out shopping, and it simply came to me. She had, for weeks, been cold, calloused, and indifferent toward me. Suddenly, I realized what the problem was. I put my children in the car and drove to Dr. Ewing's office and saw my wife coming out of his building that late afternoon. That was a Wednesday afternoon - the afternoon each week that his office is closed."

"What did you do then?"

"I returned home with the children."

"Sir, what action did you take upon learning, as you say, your wife was seeing Dr. Ewing?"

Jan Warner had obtained information back from the Legal Research Group suggesting that I should be exempt from wiretap liabilities because I lived in the home where the wiretap had been installed and my home was being invaded by an unwelcomed intruder. This was the right moment, I felt, to reveal the facts of the wiretap.

I responded, "I installed an extension phone and tapped that phone."

"So, you listened in on telephone conversations that you were not a part of and then tapped that phone?"

"Yes, sir."

"Weren't you concerned about violating federal wiretapping laws?"

"Yes, sir."

"And, so, why did you proceed?"

"My children were at stake. I knew I should be the one to remain active in their lives and it didn't matter to me whether I might be violating a law or not. Any violation of a law was secondary to the welfare of the children. As well, without evidence it would have been my word against theirs."

"You didn't use the phone provided by the telephone company?"

"No, sir."

"At that time had you conferred with a lawyer?"

"No, Sir."

"And you heard telephone calls between Dr. Ewing and your wife."

"Yes, sir."

"Was there a pattern of calls established?"

"Yes, sir. Generally, these calls occurred around ten in the mornings weekdays and one to two in the afternoons. And every night."

"And your wife did not become suspicious of your eavesdropping?"

"No, sir."

"Did anyone help you install that phone or tap?"

"No, sir."

"Do you have the ability to do something of that nature?"

"I had the basic knowledge and found it easy enough to do."

"Okay, Mr. Baumrind, did you tell anyone or your wife you had installed this device?"

"No, sir, not immediately, and I never told my wife."

"When did others learn of this?"

"After I listened to the first conversation between Dr. Ewing and my wife, I hired a private detective, and I told him about the wiretap. Then, I hired Mr. Warner and told him as well."

"All right. And, so, you heard a number of conversations following that between the two of them?"

"Yes, sir,"

"How were you able to conduct your business with all this going on?"

"Poorly" I said. "My business has suffered."

Page's tone turned disdainful.

"So, when exactly did you employ these detectives?"

"I think, sir, a couple of days after suspecting my wife was seeing Dr. Ewing."

"You think?"

"Yes, sir, the day after the revelation, I secured what I needed to tap the telephone and installed the device that night. Then the next day, after hearing the first recordings, I hired the detectives."

"So, Mr. Baumrind, when did you hire Mr. Warner?"

Jan Warner immediately asserted client-attorney privilege.

"Okay, so did you supply your attorney with information gleaned from these recordings?"

DECEIT

"I did, sir."

"Mr. Baumrind, did you coordinate information obtained from this illegal wiretap to your detectives and Mr. Warner?"

Jan Warner again asserted client-attorney privilege.

"All right, during the time that the detectives had your wife under surveillance had you contacted an attorney at all?"

"Yes, sir. I contacted Mr. Warner."

Jan had had enough. "Let me make an objection here as far as when he contacted and how he contacted his attorney. We take the position that that is an attorney-client privilege, and I don't think it's relevant as to when he hired an attorney and I'm going to instruct him not to answer anything about the attorney-client relationship. That relates to when, how or anything else."

Page looked done in, suddenly resigned, "Do you have some photographs that have been taken?"

"I'm not in possession of any photographs."

"In your attorney's possession?"

Jan objected again.

"Okay, so I presume you have some tape recordings?"

"Yes sir," I responded.

"Of conversations between whom?" said Page.

"Dr. Ewing and my wife."

"And, Mr. Baumrind, who is in possession of these tape recordings?"

"I am, sir."

I had given the tapes to Jan Warner. He had them transcribed and certified and then, returned them to me.

"Mr. Baumrind, hasn't your wife made repeated attempts to reconcile with you since these papers were served?"

"She has made two very feeble attempts. But after all that had occurred, I couldn't trust her motives and I told her so. And worse, she continued seeing Dr. Ewing and I was aware of that."

There were no further questions.

CHAPTER FIFTEEN

Within one week of James Ewing's deposition, he filed an $850,000 counter lawsuit against me for invasion of privacy as a result of the wiretap. Sixty days later, the Ewing team instigated an investigation by the FBI against me for violation of the federal wiretapping statutes, resulting in an accusation and charge of illegal wiretapping.

The two civil suits - mine against Ewing and Ewing's against me—traveled pretty much in tandem from that point on. The judge in the local judicial court ruled that the third segment of my lawsuit for malpractice should more precisely be for outrage rather than malpractice, since malpractice is the result of a negligent act, and the doctor did not commit a negligent act. Rather, he had committed a willful, outrageous act. Therefore, the charge of malpractice was supplanted by outrage as the third cause of action.

In the meantime, the custody issue with Linda proceeded with several depositions in advance of the final hearing in the family court. She and I were staunch adversaries now, although still married. We knew that she had been in constant contact with Ewing since the temporary divorce/custody hearing, although she denied this under oath. On February 21, 1979 Jan Warner received an answer and counterclaim from Linda's attorney denying all major allegations and asserting that she should be granted custody of the children with full support from me.

The divorce hearing convened April 3, 1979, in family court proceedings with Judge Dan McCann presiding. Linda looked impeccable and more beautiful than ever - goddess-like, maybe even virtuous—in an attractive yellow dress. Her motivation was to leverage her visual asset. Even though she was quite thin, she was lovely. I glanced at her. She gave me a look that said I did not exist, that we'd never met. A few minutes in, Jan Warner told me he was concerned about the judge's apparent attraction to her. This was not the start we had hoped for, but this was her advantage

Linda had one more advantage that day—in her mind, at least. This day, coincidentally, was one of Linda's visitation days with the children and shortly into the hearing, Linda's mother arrived with David and Jade. I could see my children through the door of the courtroom and noted David's discomfort. I felt this was terribly wrong to bring the children to the proceeding. It was again a demonstration of Linda's insensitivity to the children to subject them to the pressures of the court and further proof of her selfishness and dogged determination to do whatever benefited her regardless of who was being hurt. At the morning court recess the judge invited the children into his chambers. It was obvious they were going to be put in the middle—an ominous position to put a five-year old and two-year old in. I couldn't believe the court was allowing this to take place. I expressed my concern with what was occurring to Jan, and when we reconvened after the break, he placed into the record our objection to the children's appearance. However, the judge promptly commented, "Don't concern yourself—the children were impartial."

Jan Warner requested that the tapes and the transcripts of those tapes be entered into the record as evidence on behalf of the petitioner. The judge admitted them into evidence. The truth inside the tapes and transcripts would play a powerful role in the exposure of Linda's lies and, ultimately, the judge's decision. The detectives testified first with all the lurid details of each of the events that had occurred. Then I took the stand, questioned by Jan Warner. I responded with the same background details as I'd provided at the deposition: the marriage from my perspective, the developing events, when I'd first suspected my wife's illicit activities, the installation of the wiretap, and so on.

Dr. Schnackenberg's testimony followed my own. He was of the opinion that David had been affected by the affair. The child was overly shy, inhibited, frightened, and withdrawn as a result of his mother's having been distracted by the affair. Specifically, the child constantly watched the psychiatrist to see whether he met with approval or not. He was upset if he spilled anything, constantly picking up the sand his sister spilled, not spontaneous, repeating activities like smoothing out the sand over and over. While Linda had been intent on the relationship with Dr. Ewing, the children had been neglected. They were continually interfering with her telephone conversations, making her impatient with them, as she was sneaking around deceptively to talk to and meet with Ewing to their detriment. As well, Linda had a history of slapping David in the face and occasionally locking him in his room, and the psychiatrist was overly concerned about what effect that would have on the child in the long term.

Dr. Schnackenberg further stated that my two-year-old, Jade, did not have any emotional problems. On the other hand, David was frightened of any criticism, was fearful to try anything new, and had difficulty making transitions from one activity to another. This was all connected, Dr. Schnackenberg said to his mother's distraction with activities outside the home of a stressful nature, preventing her from focusing on providing a secure and comfortable home for her children. It was his position that Linda's keeping her secret and inviting the "boyfriend" into the home when the children were asleep, and "carrying on" her chosen priorities caused her stress, which leaked over to the children. As well, she had been irritable, overly controlling, and critical, requiring perfection of the children, wanting them to be little adults, rather than concentrating on their needs and letting them be children. Her illicit relationship made her less capable of being a psychologically available mother.

David had told Dr. Schnackenberg that his mother had hit both him and Jade and locked him in his room. Presumably to counter Dr. Schnackenberg's testimony, Linda had taken David to another therapist. Dr. Schnackenberg observed, however, that David felt confused about having to keep secret his seeing another therapist. When the child was asked how many doctors he was seeing, he raised one finger, and then two fingers, and then said, "It's a secret." And, on two occasions, Dr. Schnackenberg had asked Linda if she would tell him if David were seeing anyone else, and both times she stated no, he wasn't. He asked directly, "You would tell me, wouldn't you, if the child is seeing any other therapist," and she told him on both occasions, that he wasn't seeing anyone else. "Forcing a child to withhold information like this would be very stressful," the doctor said. He had "serious questions about Linda's character and her parenting skills," concerned that she would deceive him and that she "would involve her son in this deception. And taking the child to a second therapist without both therapists knowing it would jeopardize her son's therapy because he would be getting one kind of approach from one therapist and another approach from the other. No two therapists have exactly the same approach, and it would be stressful on a child to have two different approaches at the same time."

Thus, it was Dr. Schnackenberg's testimony that Linda had a self-centered attitude toward her child's therapy. He didn't "object to David having another therapist, but not dealing with the situation openly meant neither therapist knew of the other, and this behavior was consistent with the allegations about her involvement with Dr. Ewing; that she would go outside of convention to advantage herself, even to the detriment of her children and family." Given everything he had learned about the circumstances, "the whole pattern of behavior was consistent, fit, and there was nothing out of order." Despite the child's stress in seeing more than a single therapist, Dr. Schnackenberg testified that David had otherwise made great strides in the custody of his father during the previous three months between his having met the children in December 1978 and the divorce and custody hearing in April 1979.

Moreover, Linda had been required in the temporary order to meet with Dr. Schnackenberg for his analysis. However, she made it difficult for him to see her, canceling appointments at the last minute and arguing with him that there was nothing wrong with either child. After Linda's testimony, which followed mine, her attorney argued to the judge that Dr. Schnackenberg's written report on the analysis of the family was overly one-sided: highly critical of the mother but with effusive compliments for the father that seemed unfair to them. As well, her attorney expressed his concern about the correlation between the "glowing report" on the child given since the first interview as opposed to the current report three months later. As indicated previously, David had made great strides between December and April, despite the stress of seeing two therapists. Dr. Schnackenberg attributed "this to his new healthy home and the fact that he'd had three months of psychotherapy."

Linda was sworn in and testified in response to her attorney's questions as follows:

"Are you Linda Baumrind, the respondent in this action?"

"Yes."

"You are married to Vernon Baumrind?"

"Yes."

"When were you married?"

"December 23, 1967."

"Mrs. Baumrind, you have two children - David and Jade?"

"Yes."

"Will you tell me the children's ages please?"

"Jade is two-and-a-half and David is five."

"Mrs. Baumrind, did you and Mr. Baumrind seek marriage counseling sometime in late 1978?"

"Yes."

"But you stopped going to the counselor?"

"Yes, we did."

"When did you stop going to the counselor?"

"Before Christmas. It was getting to be too close to the holidays and I had a lot of baking and things to do…I think we had set up an appointment for early January."

"Did you ever become romantically involved with Dr. Ewing?"

"Well, in late December, one day at his office, yes."

"Did that relationship continue?"

"No."

"Do you deny that you've talked with Dr. Ewing since January 2nd, 1979?"

"No, I have discussed… well, he knew that I was very upset, and it was a traumatic thing for me to have the children taken away from me like they were, and he thought I was going to have a breakdown. I was upset about the children."

"Do you have any future desires with regard to Dr, Ewing?"

"No."

"Subsequent to January 2, 1979, did you discuss with your husband the possibility of reconciliation?"

"Yes."

"And did he indicate that he would take you back?"

"Well…Yes, he did."

"Have you had any discussions with him of late about reconciliation?"

"No."

"Could you reconcile with your husband?"

"After all of this, no."

So, I thought, *It's all about her! That's what this is all about - her! She's playing the role of the victim for the sympathy that provides her. Apparently, all of this activity against her was instigated, coordinated, and carried out maliciously and wrongfully by me and it was solely my fault that we were where we were in this matter… Well, her problem is the fact that truth is not her ally!*

"Do you love Dr. Ewing?"

"No."

The balance of her attorney's questions related to what she wanted from the divorce settlement: the children, various possessions, a car, support payments and alimony, to remain in the house—all the usual things.

At this point, Jan Warner cross-examined her.

"Did you tell Dr. Ewing that for him, you'd give up the house and go to work, and if you got the children, you'd put them in a daycare center?"

"No."

"Did you tell Dr. Ewing it would be a hard choice between him and the children?"

"I don't believe so."

"When did you say it was that you had an adulterous event with Dr. Ewing?"

"At the end of December." She began to cry.

"Did you commit other sexual acts with him?"

"No."

"On occasion, did you engage with him in fellatio?"

"No."

"Did you engage in cunnilingus with him? Did he engage in cunnilingus with you?"

"No."

"You deny these things?"

"Yes."

"Was one of these occasions at the park, that you and he had intercourse?"

"No."

"Let me ask you this, Mrs. Baumrind: Did you and Dr. Ewing discuss him having his wife and you engaging in sex at the same time?"

"Well…that was his idea…not my idea…I wouldn't do that."

"Now, Mrs. Baumrind, are you telling us these ideas for sex acts were Dr. Ewing's and not yours?"

"Yes."

"That Saturday in late December when you and Dr. Ewing met in his office did you perform fellatio on Dr. Ewing?"

"No."

"You deny it?"

"I could have." Tears were streaming down again.

"You don't remember that?"

"No."

"Did you have a discussion with Dr. Ewing in late December 1978 about your inability to swallow semen like he wanted you to?"

"No."

Jan showed Linda photographs of the interior of the house—David's room, Jade's, the den, photographs that made it clear that Jade's room in particular was closely located to the area in the den where she and Ewing had had their "meeting" that night of December 30th. She confirmed the photos to be accurate.

"Now, Mrs. Baumrind, can you show us in these photos where exactly in the house you met with Dr. Ewing?"

She pointed to the den.

"Can you show us where the children were in the house?"

She pointed to the children's rooms.

"Did you stay on the telephone with Dr. Ewing three, four and five times a day from October through December 1978?"

"No."

"You deny that?"

"Yes."

"In the month of December, how many times did you talk to him per day?"

"It wouldn't be every day. All right, on the day that he called, maybe once, maybe twice. I'm not sure. I don't remember exactly how many times."

"Was it at his office that you had these two sexual acts with him?"

"Yes."

"So, did you not have sexual intercourse with him in the park?"

"No."

"Let me ask you this. On Saturday, December 16th, was that the time you had intercourse with Dr. Ewing at his office?"

"I don't know what date it was."

"You don't know. Wasn't this important to you in going outside your marital vows to have a relationship with a man who was not your husband? It wasn't important to you to remember when that was."

"I was upset about it."

"Upset about it then also?"

"Yes."

"Was it December 23rd, the Saturday you went to his office, yours and Mr. Baumrind's eleventh wedding anniversary?"

"I don't know."

"Your wedding anniversary date and you wouldn't remember that you were having sexual intercourse with a man to whom you were not married, on your wedding anniversary?"

"It could have been."

"Again, on December 30th, when you went to his office on Saturday morning at 10:15, you had intercourse again that morning, didn't you?"

"Maybe."

"You and Dr. Ewing agreed you'd continue to lie to your husband until you could put him out of the house, is that correct?"

"I don't believe so, no."

"Mrs. Baumrind, do you remember talking to Dr. Ewing and telling him if you were looking for material things, you would be happy with Vernon, but that's not what you were looking for?"

"I don't remember."

"Didn't you tell him it was just about going to kill Vernon when you put him out and took his children from him? You remember telling him that?"

"No."

"You deny you told Dr. Ewing that?"

"These conversations are four months ago. I don't know exactly. I don't remember, so much has happened. I've been in such a state of depression, I don't know."

"Were you in a state of depression while you were talking to Dr. Ewing all during this time and seeing him at these two times you've admitted?"

"I was upset because of marital problems, yes."

"If your husband, on coming home, would approach the entry door, you'd hang up on Dr. Ewing, wouldn't you?"

"I don't know. If it was supper time and I was on the phone with anybody, I'd hang up because he was home, and supper was ready."

"On the 13th of December 1978, you and Dr. Ewing planned for him to sneak in the back way for him to come to the house on the 21st when your husband was to be out of town. Is that correct?"

"I don't know."

"Do you remember Dr. Ewing asking you if you thought it was a trap for him to come over on the 14th? Do you remember that?"

"I don't know."

"Do you remember telling him you could lock the doors, put the deadbolts on, or you could get a babysitter, maybe even your friend Susan Johnson, who had indicated she would babysit for you while you and Dr. Ewing went somewhere? Do you remember that?"

"I doubt it."

"Do you deny that, Mrs. Baumrind?"

"Well, I just don't know."

"You don't remember?"

"No."

"Do you remember telling Dr. Ewing your friend, Susan Johnson, was a screwball?"

"I don't know, maybe I jokingly said that."

"Susan is kind of crazy, but you would trust her, isn't that right?"

"Yes."

"Didn't you tell Dr. Ewing you would not be embarrassed if you got caught in bed with him by your husband, isn't that what you told Dr. Ewing?"

"I don't know."

"You deny it, Mrs. Baumrind?"

"I don't know if I said that or not."

"You don't know if you said it?"

"I don't remember."

"Would it help if you looked at the written transcriptions?"

"No. You could have just written it up that way, just like the lying detectives and what they have said."

"Would it help you to listen to the tape-recorded conversation?"

"How would I know that was my voice on there?"

At this point, the judge asked, "You're not denying these conversations, are you?"

"I talked with him, but I don't know exactly what I told him."

"Mrs. Baumrind, did you tell Dr. Ewing that if your husband came home, he could jump out the bathroom window? Do you remember that?"

She laughed at this question. "Now, I don't remember that."

"Mrs. Baumrind, is there something funny about this?"

"No, but you just … I don't know exactly what I said."

"Mrs. Baumrind, you know that your husband has a great deal of love for these children, don't you?"

"We both do."

"Did you tell Dr. Ewing on the 20th, when he asked you if you'd give up the house, you said that's all right with me. And then you said, that's what you get for sin? You remember that?"

"Possibly, I don't know."

"Mrs. Baumrind, you denied having intercourse with Dr. Ewing in your home December 21st, 1978, when your husband was out of town. Is that correct? Do you remember that?"

"Yes."

"Well, can you tell us, then, did you discuss with Dr. Ewing your husband coming home and finding Dr. Ewing's red pubic hairs on the rug?"

"I don't think we discussed that at all."

"You don't remember that?"

"I deny that."

"Were you in love with Dr. Ewing?"

"No."

"You told Dr. Ewing you'd had problems with Mr. Baumrind since you married him? Is that right?"

"No, I wouldn't say that, no."

"Now, Mrs. Baumrind, you discussed with him you and him and his wife or some other woman engaging in sex at the same time?"

"Well, if that was mentioned, that was his idea. That wouldn't be my idea."

"Didn't you tell him you'd do it if it made him happy?"

"I wouldn't do that."

"Didn't he ask you about performing sex acts on him with other people watching, performing fellatio on him with other people watching and didn't you tell him if that made him happy, you'd do it?"

"I wouldn't do that."

"Did you engage in fellatio with Dr. Ewing?"

"No."

At this point Linda's attorney interrupted the questioning, stating to the judge, "I believe they've beat this thing to death, this relationship between the two. I think my client has done the best she can. She's admitted she's had a relationship with him. I don't think Mr. Warner is doing anything here but loading up the record with various and sundry things that I see no value for."

The judge responded, "I think he can ask that question" the judge responded. It's a proper question."

So, Jan repeated, "Did you have fellatio with Dr. Ewing?"

"We didn't plan on any definite sex. I explained it just happened."

"That Saturday in late December, did you perform fellatio on Dr. Ewing?"

"I don't remember."

"Didn't you have a discussion with Dr. Ewing on December 27th, 1978, about your inability to swallow his semen like he wanted you to?"

"I don't think it was ever said like you're saying it."

"You don't remember telling him you'd do it, if it made him happy?"

"No."

"If I read it to you, would you remember it?"

"No, that could be all lies, like I said."

"All these times you talked with Dr. Ewing was within the confines of the kitchen where the telephone was, is that right?"

"Yes. It's our only phone in the house, until Vernon installed that illegal phone upstairs."

"Mrs. Baumrind, you just don't remember any of these conversations, do you?"

"No."

"You remember verbatim what happened between you and your husband from the time he got out of the Navy, and you can't remember what you said on the telephone, what did you say, less than four months ago, is that right?"

"I don't remember phone conversations."

"So, you're following Dr. Ewing's advice that he gave you, when he told you, 'If you don't want them to know something, just say you don't remember it.' Is that what you're doing?"

"I don't think so."

"Mrs. Baumrind, as far as slapping your son, how many times have you slapped him in the face?"

"Very rarely."

"What would prompt you to slap a five-year-old child in the face?"

"If he answered me back sharply, I may have given him a little tap on the face. I think every parent has done that."

"A tap on the face?"

"Or a slap for having a nasty mouth, yes."

As I heard this response, I thought, *So, why would you not be slapping Ewing around for his repulsive comments and abhorrent behavior?* It was almost impossible for me to understand how she could not have been turned off by Ewing's filthy conversations; instead she had been attracted to this behavior. It will always be impossible to understand.

"You denied to Dr. Moran, the therapist you took the boy to, that you had slapped him in the face, didn't you?"

"I don't know. I don't remember. It's not a regular habit of mine to slap them in the face".

"But you did, if you got mad?"

"Yeah, I would say so, yes."

"You heard the therapist testify about your son. Every other answer he gave on this thing was about getting a spanking; Mommy giving him a spanking. That was the doctor you hired, wasn't it?"

"Yes."

"You hired that doctor to evaluate these children, didn't you?"

"Yes, but I also think that David could be programmed to say that. He's only been in my presence in the last three months, thirty hours a week. I don't know what they're telling him, drilling into him, hearing all these lies from your side. He could be programmed to say Mommy slaps you when you go to Momma's house."

"Mrs. Baumrind, will you admit that there is no fault, alleged, or testified to, of your husband as far as these children are concerned? There's no moral failure on his part?"

"Moral fault?"

The judge interjected. "I haven't heard anyone say anything about any moral fault on the part of Mr. Baumrind. Do you want to pick one up?"

"No sir." Jan responded.

The judge said, "Well… don't say anything about it, then."

Jan continued. "Let me ask you this, Mrs. Baumrind. You say you didn't have any sexual activity in the park in late December."

"Right."

"You just sat there and talked?"

"I don't remember exactly."

"Didn't you tell the doctor if you saw the detectives again the next morning when you got together with him at his office, as you and he planned, that you would wave at them from his balcony?"

"Well, I had seen some men who told me they were detectives. I don't know."

"So, after all that happened in the park on Friday, December 29th, knowing you had likely been under surveillance, you and Doctor Ewing still determined to meet the next morning to resume your activities together? In spite of all that?"

"I didn't know if I was being followed exactly."

"But you were suspicious, weren't you?"

"Yes. I thought maybe I was. Nothing went on. I didn't know. I don't know if the next day was the day we met."

"Why is it, Mrs. Baumrind, not one tear was shed at your deposition, but today, I think I've counted five times you've broken down?" This question was posed to counter the effect of Linda's tears on the judge.

"I don't know."

"No further questions, Your Honor."

The coup de grace in the custody issue was her continued contact with Ewing after the service of the order on that Tuesday, January 2nd. It demonstrated a blatant disregard for rule of law, and life's fundamental principles and morals. Suspecting her continued contact with Ewing, I kept the detectives engaged at times they and I thought she and Ewing would reconnect. Sure enough they did, and this was documented for testimony in the family court, all helpful in the custody matter.

The judge, then, proceeded to go over a four-page list of personal property with Linda to determine which items she was claiming as hers from the marital home. The list included practically everything we owned. Jan Warner and I had decided I would not ask for anything. This would make it clear that nothing was more important to me than custody of my children.

After Linda had finished going over her list in detail, Jan Warner turned to the judge, "I'd like the record to reflect that the court has gone through a four-page list with this lady," he said. "She had no problem remembering everything about the items on this list that were purchased ten to eleven years ago. Let the record show that there was no problem with her memory."

Following Linda's testimony, her attorney introduced Dr. Moran, who had arrived late to the hearing. They had hastily hired this doctor as a witness to counter Dr. Schnackenberg's testimony. The hearing was near its end, and Linda's attorney had not had an opportunity to have any pre-hearing discussion with Dr. Moran. As a late entry for the defense, the doctor introduced himself as a forensic psychiatrist. His credentials and recital of experience in court testimony and evaluation of clients was impressive. We were thus surprised to hear him state that, in his opinion, the morals of a woman should not be considered as relevant criteria in judging her ability to be a good mother. He did not believe a mother teaches morals and values out of the milieu of her own philosophy, or that her own lifestyle would set an example for her children. He testified that he had concluded that Linda was of fit character to have custody of her children, and he advised that he had arrived at this decision from materials he had read in connection with the case which had been supplied by Linda's attorney.

At the conclusion of Dr. Moran's testimony, Jan Warner asked him if he believed the children were not emotionally stable and secure. He stated that he believed they were from the material he had studied. He had only met with Linda and the children once. Without mentioning who had custody of the children, Jan then asked whether he felt the children should be left in the home in which they currently resided. Dr. Moran responded that he did, whereupon Jan said, "Thank you, sir, that will be all." Dr. Moran's testimony was over.

We were stunned that Linda's psychiatrist had committed a grave error. He had unwittingly played right into Jan's hand. His late arrival had handicapped him, and he apparently did not have a clear understanding of all the issues, as he did not know which party had custody of the children. He had just admitted that the children were in good hands and should remain where they were—with me! That was disastrous for the defendant.

The hearing ended, and now we had to wait for the judge's decision which was expected within a week or two.

CHAPTER SIXTEEN

In the state of South Carolina at that time, it was possible to obtain a divorce on grounds of adultery within ninety days. On this day, April 17, 1979, 105 days from the day Linda was served with papers, the family court judge rendered his decision in the Baumrind vs Baumrind matter. Jan Warner called with good news: the divorce was final, and I had been awarded custody of the children. Justice had been served, and the welfare of the children had been placed in my hands. The written final order of the court would be delivered to me within days. I was ecstatic with the outcome, of course, and grateful for the strength I had been granted to take the actions I had been forced to take.

But I could not rejoice for Linda's loss. I knew how devastating this was for her, and I felt very sorry for her. Regardless of all that had transpired, regardless of her personal preferences, in spite of all that was to be, I still could not let go of the past emotionally. Unlike her, it was impossible for me to have lived with her for eleven years and then abruptly cut off any feelings for her, as she had for me with his entry into her life. For me, a divorce decree did not automatically end the ties we had. The children - the greatest gift any of us ever receives—and our common goals, dreams, family, friends, all we had accomplished together and shared were all attachments that were impossible to simply sever despite the events. My feelings would persist. She had none. Thankful for the win, regardless, I determined to get on with mine and the children's lives.

The final order stated the rules of custody as follows:

It Be So Ordered:

1. That the Petitioner is thereby granted a complete and final divorce of and from the Respondent upon the grounds of adultery.
2. That the Petitioner is granted custody of the two minor children of the marriage·, namely, David Baumrind and Jade Baumrind.
3. That the Respondent is entitled to visitation with said children within the state, as follows: Every other weekend from Friday at 5:00 PM until Sunday at 5:00 PM. The respondent is to pick up the children from the residence where they reside. The Respondent has the right to visit with the children for one week before Christmas and up through Christmas Eve at 7:00. During the summer months, the Respondent has the right to visit with the children for two weeks during June (second and third weeks from 5:00 PM on Friday until 5:00 on Friday) and two weeks during August (also from Friday to Friday).
4. That the Respondent is denied any and all alimony, maintenance, and attorney's fees.
5. That the Petitioner is to purchase Respondent's interest in and to the jointly held residence as set forth herein within ninety days.

6. That the Petitioner is to transfer to the Respondent, free and clear of liens and encumbrances, the Buick titled in his name.
7. That Petitioner is to maintain title to the Buick station wagon and pay on the lien therein.
8. That the Petitioner is from this day forward to have no obligation to the Respondent of any nature or description and is to be responsible for no obligation incurred by her since the separation of the parties on January 2, 1979.
9. That certified copies of the Decree are to be forwarded to counsel for each of the parties, the same to constitute proper service.

And So It Is Ordered.

The transcripts of the wiretapped recordings had proven Linda lied to the court. Morality had been deemed an appropriate factor in whether she was a capable parent. Linda's own psychiatrist, Dr. Moran, had agreed that David had apparently made great strides in his present environment. Despite the initial apparent attraction the judge had for Linda, with the weight of all the evidence, including all the facts and testimony and the credibility of the parties and their witnesses, there was little to no choice for the judge but to conclude that the best interests of the children was with the father who was the "more fit, proper, and suitable custodian."

As stated in the divorce decree, dated April 24, 1979, "There was no question but that the breakup of the marriage was totally the fault of the respondent. It was apparent that the respondent made little, if any, (financial) contribution during the marriage. Respondent is a schoolteacher, whose certificate could be renewed, and she is well capable of employment. There had been no allegation that the respondent was unhealthy and could not work."

As I viewed the order, a tide of monumental sadness washed over me. Reflecting eleven years, I thought about standing at the altar, pronouncing my wedding vows, sincerely and prayerfully, in a church full of friends and family. I had taken my vows seriously and the words that joined us permanently. I put all my hopes, dreams, and ambitions into what lay ahead that December 23rd, 1967.

I thought, *how quickly life can turn around!* In what seemed to be a moment (relatively) of senseless irresponsibility, the good times were over. Our family had been torn apart. The children and I would journey forward without their mother. It was heart-breaking. There was no changing the circumstances; no turning back, no denial that the events hadn't happened. I remained in disbelief that she had been unwilling to put her heart and soul into trying to get her family back, and I felt awful about the fact that I had to instigate the divorce process, having commenced that effort from a very fragile beginning.

I had always believed it possible to turn a seemingly lost cause into a triumph. I'd done it often in business. I enjoyed the challenge. But, in this case, I couldn't overcome Linda's closed mind and lost conscience. I thought, *her death would have been more acceptable than the dishonor of this behavior.* It was ironic that I could have the strength and resolve to overcome the odds of a judicial system that for ages had been biased in favor of the mother and, yet I had not had the strength and power to save our family for all the reasons a family should survive. I was powerless in withstanding Ewing's intrusion, his influence on Linda, and her attraction to him in total disregard of her marital and family commitments.

The entire experience had been like that of the long-distance runner who, at the back of the pack, reaches way down from within himself and comes up with that extra herculean effort to cross the finish line ahead of all competitors. Justice had been served and that doesn't always happen. So I counted myself lucky in that regard. But I'd had an excellent attorney and the behavior of Linda and Ewing had been so abysmal that they had been "unable to catch up with us," just as Jan Warner had prophesied.

Over a period of twelve years following the divorce and initial custody hearing, there were five attempts to regain custody, none successful, but all coming at great expense, both emotionally and financially.

After the custody hearing and before the alienation trial in late May 1979, Linda called and asked to come by the house. She stopped by on a Saturday afternoon. Due to the same persistent emotional bond I'd had with her in the past, I felt I had to leave a literal and figurative door open for the possibility of a miracle to occur, although I would not jeopardize my legal position with the children. While David and Jade played in the backyard, she and I sat on the backsteps and talked - the same backstep entrance that Ewing had entered the night I had gone to Columbia to meet Dr. Schnackenberg the first time, the night he and Linda had their "meeting" on the carpet in front of our den fireplace with the children sleeping close by.

For the first time, we were not two angry, threatened, and threatening opponents. There were no judgments, no accusations, no recriminations, and no resurrection of recent history. We maintained straight dialogue - just feelings for what we shared together, although I still could not know of her sincerity or of her true motivations. That kind of conversation was what had been needed so badly for months: a wholesome conversation void of all the negatives that had pervaded our lives since the fall of 1978.

The presumed purpose of this meeting was to discuss our "common interests," Linda had said. She said we'd had a lot in common and that, in the interests of the children, we should explore the possibilities of reconciling. I knew well that reconciling would require more of her than she likely was capable; but I wanted to always remain open to the possibilities, without giving up my advantages. In the discussion, she told me that she had "just been existing", that it was "just romance" between her and Ewing, and that she "had a good husband" and had "thrown it all away." She asked me to think about our conversation and to call her. After our discussion, I invited Linda to have dinner with me and the children. We ate out together and afterwards she departed. It could have been a new beginning.

But, three nights later, following my suspicions that she had again not been sincere with me, I drove by Ewing's new office building he had just built for his practice. I parked on the street and walked up to a front window. It was dark outside. The building was lit up. Ewing was in his private office and Linda was with him. She was helping him hang pictures on the wall. I knocked on the window so that she would know I had seen her. She turned and saw me, turned her back to me and continued with what she was doing as though I was not there. That night, she became a complete stranger to me.

She might have had a lot of other shortcomings, but Linda was a survivor. She was a strong individual and apparently had accepted her predicament - at least temporarily - until she could regroup for another struggle to file suit to reverse custody, I expected. At that point, I knew for certain that her motives with me were entirely hostile; and all-the-while she had only been trying to deceive me, just as she had done from the inception of her relationship with Ewing.

As required by the divorce decree, Linda was to pick up and deliver the children back to our home during her visitation times. This was the way it was throughout the years, but on a single occasion, as an accommodation to her, since I was passing nearby at the time she would have had to leave with the children to deliver them back home, I called her and suggested I'd be glad to pick them up to save her the 45 mile round trip. Upon my arrival, the children were ready and I put them in their car seats, returning to Linda's front porch to retrieve their suitcases from their weekend's visit with her. As I retrieved their suitcases and started toward my car with the children strapped into their seats, Linda blurted out at me, "I'll hate you forever for hiring that goddamn Jew lawyer and that lying psychiatrist…You know, Vernon, sex is important!" I've never given her an opportunity alone with me again to express her animosity like that.

Jimmy and Louise Ewing divorced in October 1980, and on December 6, 1980, Ewing married Linda. My children took part in the ceremony with a justice of the peace. Linda had coordinated their wedding with a day she was scheduled to have the children. In late December, I learned the newlyweds had bought a home in the very subdivision I developed in Florence among the remaining lots I had to build on in the subdivision and homes I had under construction at that time. I could only assume they were flaunting themselves in my face and/or were hoping this strategy would cause me to do something irrational that would give them an advantage in an anticipated attempt to regain custody. Although they were accomplishing their objective of making life more difficult for me, I determined to be bigger than them. Also, my children were put in the middle again, and it would be difficult and confusing for them if I didn't take the high road. I couldn't avoid being in the subdivision often. In one way or another, we all were bound to run into one another; and we did.

On January 14, 1981, within weeks of Linda's marriage to Ewing, she called, telling me it was important that we meet and speak. Recognizing her pattern of conveying a false sign of encouragement, a deceptive ray of hope, and then, dashing the expectations by reality, I told her I was not interested in having any conversation with her, unless it dealt strictly with our children. We personally met the next day at Timrod Park, a very public place, and I sat in her car with her. The meeting was very brief. She proceeded to tell me what I had heard before, that it had just been a romantic thing with Ewing, that she would divorce him, if I would take her back. She wanted a commitment from me. This was the usual Quid Pro Quo offer from her I'd become accustomed to; nothing new, nothing of substance and nothing convincing. I told her I wasn't bargaining with her; that she couldn't keep two men dangling on opposite ends of a string while she vacillated back and forth from one to the other. With that, I opened the door on my side of the car and got out. That was the end for me, and nothing like this ever happened again.

CHAPTER SEVENTEEN

Before the alienation trial could begin, the wiretap issue had to be resolved. The doctor's lawyers were asking the court to suppress the tapes as evidence based on their claim that the evidence was obtained by an illegal wiretap. As well, Ewing's attorneys had instigated an action against me for violation of the federal wiretapping statutes. This accusation was pending, and the legality or non-legality of the issue had to be settled before the suit against Ewing could proceed. At the time, violations of the federal wiretapping law were punishable by imprisonment of up to five years and both criminal and civil fines of up to $10,000.

In September 1979, Judge John Hamilton Smith of the 12th Circuit Court of South Carolina ruled the tapes were legally obtained and could be used in the alienation trial. He denied Ewing's countersuit against me, citing a case that suggested wiretapping laws were "not intended to intrude into marital relationships within the marital home." Ewing appealed Judge Smith's ruling to the South Carolina Supreme Court in early 1980.

The wiretap issue (Ewing vs Baumrind) was addressed by the South Carolina State Supreme Court which held "that the husband's conduct, under the circumstances that exist, is beyond the grasp of the federal (wiretap) statute."

While the position of the Supreme Court was that wiretaps between spouses living apart are illegal, Mrs. Baumrind and Dr. Ewing had "limited expectations of privacy" in this case. The court ruled unanimously that

1. The wiretap had been installed in the home in which the defendant (Baumrind) was still living, the wiretap was installed on wires within the home of the defendant,
2. The plaintiff in this action, Dr. Ewing, was not entitled to privacy within the confines of the defendant's home wherein he had invaded the home to seduce the defendant's wife.
3. The defendant may have been defenseless without the ability to produce incontrovertible evidence without the wiretap.

The South Carolina Supreme Court concluded that federal courts have applied varying interpretations to wiretap provisions of the law and he warned that the wiretapping in this case might have been illegal if it had not been done in the couple's home where the respondent was still living.

Dr. Ewing appealed the decision of the state Supreme Court to the Federal Supreme Court by way of a Writ of Certiorari, an appeal to a higher court. The federal Supreme Court denied the writ, essentially siding with the lower court, remanding the case back to the state for dispensation. With the denial of the Writ of Certiorari by the US Supreme Court, the charges in the pending action for violations against the federal wiretapping statutes were dropped. Initially the alienation trial judge had rendered two major pre-trial decisions; one, a stay of the litigation for the decision by higher authority in the wiretap issue and, two, the substitution of "Outrage" as the third cause of action, rather than "Malpractice." With the wiretap issue resolved and the Ewing vs. Baumrind lawsuit dismissed, the Baumrind vs. Ewing trial could proceed.

On September 14, 1981, in an open courtroom in Florence, South Carolina, the lawsuit, Baumrind vs Ewing, proceeded in the Court of Common Pleas. The judge had not yet taken the bench. The sound in the courtroom was hushed like the calm in the eye of a hurricane. Coverage of the event was widespread in South Carolina newspapers; but not the Florence paper. The Ewing defense team had been able to secure a blackout of news coverage locally; but papers with wider distributions in Columbia and Charleston carried the story, as did other papers around the country in New Orleans, San Francisco, New York, Chicago and elsewhere. The trial extended five consecutive days.

Divorce attorneys nationwide had followed the progress of the wiretap issue for the advantage it was thought to offer them in justifying wiretapping, citing Ewing vs Baumrind and the refusal of the federal court to hear the Writ of Certiorari as a precedent setting case in South Carolina which had permitted a defendant to wiretap a spouse with immunity. The case was thought to provide the legal basis for wiretapping in similar instances. Some newspaper accounts were interested in the intrigue of "interspousal espionage," or legal telephone wiretaps by husbands or wives to spy on one another. Other news accounts were more interested in "this new dimension for couples who have complained for years about being bugged by each other." And it wasn't long before scriptwriters, dramatists and the national networks were soliciting the opportunity to relate the story for "the power of its melodrama content."

VERNON BAUMRIND

It could have been royalty (except for the plaintiff) that was in attendance at trial - The Honorable Sidney T. Floyd, presiding Judge; for the Defense, Robert L. Page, Esquire, Edward: J. Dennis IV, Esquire, Eugene Zeigler, Esquire (former South Carolina State Senator), and James H. Ewing, M.D and his new wife, Linda-Sue Ewing. At the prosecution table was Jan L. Warner, Esquire, and Jan's associate attorney, C. Dixon Lee, III, and Vernon E. Baumrind, Plaintiff.

At issue was an alienation of affection/criminal conversation/outrage trial, Vernon Baumrind, Plaintiff vs. James H. Ewing, M.D., individually and as a Professional Association. Ewing had apparently "absconded with Baumrind's wife." At the defense table was the accused doctor in question, who sat there like a kind of self-satisfied egotist who knew the righteousness of living by the credo, "love conquers all." His wife Linda, the former Mrs. Baumrind, sat by his side in support with a huge new ring on her finger, glowing and beautiful with an equally complacent air about her.

There had already been notable public opinions bandied about regarding this trial on both sides of the issue. With Jan Warner at the prosecution table, I knew I was in the best of legal hands, but some of the news accounts had me somewhat uncomfortable and feeling like there were some people in the courtroom there for the sole purpose of seeing "the creep" who wiretapped his wife's telephone conversations with her paramour doctor, to see the wife, herself, and the doctor whose sexual exploits were actually captured on tape and plastered about in the newspapers and on TV across the country. You would have thought enough had already been heard of these things. This was the culmination of several years of legal wranglings over the wiretap and its contents, the progress of which had been widely publicized.

Principle had already triumphed over grief in the domestic issue in 1979 and I had already accomplished my greatest goal in all of this in the custody hearing; but the bills on all of these legal issues stemming from the domestic-custody litigations, Ewing's lawsuit against me, and the costs of defending the pending Federal Wiretapping Statute issue accumulated to over $350,000, and, for that reason, the outcome of this trial had become more important to me than it was in the beginning of the lawsuit.

Emotions were bursting inside of me like skyrockets. The long struggle against Ewing was about to begin. There were differences of opinions prior to the trial by the general public as to whether this lawsuit was justified or should have even been allowed. Some people were of the opinion that the defendant should have been "man enough," like in other places in the world, to have taken care of matters himself rather than dragging this issue into the public domain where the contents of these sensitive conversations were being publicized as a spectacle.

The jury selected was supposed to be a sampling of our peers in the community and it was hoped that the system of justice would render a fair verdict. The trial extended five days. At the heart of the issue was the content of the tape-recorded conversations between the two adulterers. There were twenty-one cassette tapes that had resulted from the wiretap and a transcript of those tapes that had been transcribed for submission in both the domestic issue and the alienation trial. The line of questioning posed to each of the parties at trial pretty much followed that of the depositions in advance of the trial. Jan Warner showed the plaintiff a box containing the tapes to be identified into evidence. As well, the transcript of the tapes was entered into evidence. The defense objected to the transcripts on the basis that they may not be accurate and there were places where the tapes were inaudible, and the transcriber stated she could not tell what was being said. At the insistence of the defense, stunningly, the tapes themselves were declared to be the better source of evidence. As such, the tapes were played in court from beginning to end extending two full days.

The essence of the plaintiff's case was that Dr. Ewing had played a major role in the breakup of the marriage with the use of his skillful knowledge and his understanding of the psychology of women. He had gained information from the plaintiff's wife in the guise of professional practice, and he used it to manipulate her to his advantage and to alienate her from the plaintiff.

Countering this contention, Dr. Ewing testified at trial stating, "Oh, Mr. Baumrind is a lot more handsome than I am!" But what did he have to offer her? He had to offer her a "Bad Boy" persona and pleasures she never knew before. And he kept bringing it up to her, and he kept calling her. He kept demeaning and degrading her husband. And under the pressure of Dr. Ewing, she felt dissatisfied with her current husband. Dr. Ewing acknowledged in the tapes, "I tried to draw y'all apart; I feel responsible." The tape-recorded conversations of Linda and Ewing bore that out; the fact that she made the decision to separate in early to mid-December 1978, during the torrid pace of her affair, was evident. The marriage got ruined.

The Defendant had no defense except to attack the Plaintiff which was done vigorously; attempting to portray the Plaintiff as cruel and heartless for taking the children away from their mother and for bringing all of this misfortune upon himself.

Jan Warner's closing arguments summed up the plaintiff's case:

"If it pleases the court, Mr. Foreman and Ladies and Gentlemen, I've been the recipient of misdirection in the past. You know, there's an old saying amongst lawyers that if you don't have the facts in your favor, argue the law. If you don't have the law on your side, argue the facts. If you don't have either one of them in your favor, pick on one of the parties. Well, in this case, the defense has had no choice but to pick on my client. You know, this divorce Dr. Ewing's three attorneys have been arguing these past five days should have been kept quiet and handled privately between the parties. Unfortunately, we have children involved here and my client had no choice but to take the action he did; and it is immensely naïve to think he should have done otherwise.

Ladies and Gentlemen, let's not worry about what these opposing lawyers say or what their clients have said. In evidence, look at the divorce decree of Doctor Ewing's divorce. I'd like you to look at it. It's part of the evidence. Here it is. I was not involved in the doctor's divorce, by the way. But look at his divorce decree. Look at the former Mrs. Baumrind's divorce decree. You're going to find that the Baumrind divorce case was tried in the family court. You're going to find that the judge who issued that decree found that the present Mrs. Ewing had a problem telling the truth. You're going to see in that decree that the former Mrs. Baumrind had a continuing relationship with this doctor despite what she had testified to. She made no appeal of the decree that was issued. That's going to tell you why the children are with my client. How could they do this to this woman? How could they snatch these children, as Dr. Ewing's attorneys would have you believe? Ladies and Gentlemen, you know, the days of snatching children are over. When the judge says they go, they go. And it's based on a showing of facts. And I'd like you to look at that decree; at how she lied to the psychiatrist. The court stipulated she was to see the psychiatrist with these children. Look at how she hired two and three more psychologists trying to get one to support her position in this case. The defense didn't tell you about those half-truths. How this little child, the one she wants so badly, with their attempt to make this big show that this man doesn't care for these children because he brings this suit. How this one little kid, this little boy, is preoccupied with being beaten and stricken by his mother. It's in there. It's not appealed. It's the facts. It's the law in this case. This divorce case is over. We're not talking about the divorce case here. What I say is, they can talk about the children, they can talk about my client, they can talk about me. My client didn't want his children exposed to that man sitting at the table with my client's ex-wife. And I really can't blame him. And the judge in this divorce case couldn't blame him either.

And what have they got now? This doctor who is broke is financing another custody suit trying to take these children away from their father who has overwhelmingly demonstrated his fitness to parent these children full time. And you heard more from this woman today about her children and her love for her children. But you know, it was Christmastime. I picked up on that and I hope you picked up on that Christmas music in the background on those raunchy tapes. Beautiful Christmas music in the background and this doctor is spewing filth and she's expressing little exception. These tapes are going back with you in the jury room. I wouldn't listen to them again. They're disgusting. Christmas music in the background. These little kids are happy. What's this lady doing? She's hanging on the telephone talking to her lover about their secretive meetings. Get out of here, kids! Shut up before I slap you. Get out; oh, wait a minute, I've got to get these kids something. I'm sorry, I kept you waiting, Jimmy. This is a woman who cares about her kids? The judge took care of the children. And I can't really blame my client, Mr. Baumrind, for not wanting his children around this man.

You know, they brought in a psychiatrist for this trial whose sole objective was to try and convince you that this man, Doctor Ewing, is not a pervert. Why did he pay $600 to this doctor for that testimony? You know, these doctors are a fraternity. They all say, my name is Dr. James H. Ewing, M.D.; what is your name. My name is Doctor Bjorksten, MD. Them fellows ain't Jim Jones or Frank Smith. They are doctors - medical doctors. Paid $600 to hear what that man had to say, which was basically nothing. I am a doctor. I'm trying to help my doctor friend here, my brethren. I don't think he convinced not one of us here in this courtroom today that this garbage we've been listening to is not perverted filth.

And, you know, Ladies and Gentlemen, we have in this society, and it's not all bad, they can quote the Bible, we have in this society, crimes. Adultery is a crime. It's punishable by imprisonment under our Criminal Code. These attorneys here today are saying, sanction it. Everybody ought to commit adultery if they want to. Everybody ought to get on the phone and talk the way these two people talked if they want to. Marriage is not sacred if they don't feel like it. Ladies and Gentlemen, marriage is a contract. The State honors marriage contracts. The State of South Carolina is interested in keeping people together. It is a very precious right. A husband and wife's right is precious.

These lawyers representing Dr. Ewing talk about chattels in this case; and I was very interested in Dr. Ewing's attorney's argument about women being chattels. Do you know who the chattels are in this case? The chattels are the doctor's poor ex-wife who he's been miserable with for years, just existing with. It says in these tapes he can't get it at home, I don't want it at home, I want you. He gets rid of what he characterized as his overweight, totally unacceptable wife. She's a chattel, an old coat. Throw her away. Get rid of her. And, then he complains.

Who's the other chattel in this case? Here he is, right here beside me. She says to him, look - not to him - she didn't say nothing to him until she knew he found out. She said, look, doctor, you know we get along great. You know, I have never been exposed to all these sexual things that you're telling me about on the telephone. And, you know, I'm just dissatisfied with my husband. I think I'll go ahead and leave him after the first of the year. It was mid-December when she made this decision. It's in the tapes - her admission is right there for all to see.

And I tell you the truth of this case is not what this lady said on the stand today. That's not the truth. In these tapes, that's where the truth lies. When you and I talk when no one is listening, or when we think no one is listening, that's when we express our innermost thoughts and feelings; from the innermost confines of our minds. That's the truth.

This lady says she had all these problems. She's a veteran witness now. She knows her agenda and what she should say now. Again, look at that divorce decree. Read what the judge said. The judge found she was unbelievable; her credibility was devoid. He found, as a matter of fact, that every time she says she doesn't remember, she doesn't want to tell you about it. You know, her memory of Mr. Baumrind's shortcomings has increased as time has gone on. Her recollection of what she heard Monday, Tuesday and Wednesday in this courtroom decreased. Her recollection of what she and Doctor Ewing did decreased. She didn't want to tell you the truth, as she has not told the truth here and it is in writing on the records of this court that she did not tell the truth.

Mr. Foreman, Ladies and Gentlemen, in society, there are people we look up to. We think doctors walk on water. We look up to ministers. We intend that if we go to a minister to confide in this minister our innermost feelings, the minister is not going to talk about it to others. We want the minister to help us. And, if it's my wife, or anybody's wife or husband, we don't expect that minister to have an attraction to our spouse and end up taking our spouse from us after he has gathered all the necessary information and made a judgment call. You know, ministers and doctors are knowledgeable in psychology. They know how to use it. And we expect doctors to be trustworthy. You know, all ladies go to gynecologists. They've got to go. My wife goes. Doctor Ewing's attorneys' wives go. Everybody's wife has to go. I do not expect my wife to go to a gynecologist, a board-certified gynecologist, or any gynecologist, who will sit there and look at her, thinking, boy, that's a good-looking number, and I'm not real happy at home. Let me think about this a little bit. I want my wife to go to someone who she can trust, who I can trust. I submit to you the question of filth, it turned my stomach, and it still does. To think about it, because I think about my wife possibly going to some doctor like this who is doing nothing but sizing up his prey, when he has a higher obligation.

So, look at the decree. Mr. Baumrind was found not to be at fault in the cause of the separation. This lady had a perfect opportunity to testify to anything she wanted to in the divorce-custody matter. Everything she has said bad about this man today I've never heard this stuff before today. Never heard it, in all the child custody litigation that preceded this alienation trial, and she was fighting for her children then. And I've been involved in the divorce case from the beginning.

The suggestion by the defense that my client's action is frivolous and inconsequential is ludicrous. We're here because the law says we're entitled to be here. We're here because we're damaged. And who better to tell you about the damages than these purveyors and initiators of filth? Them. What does she say and what does he say in the tapes about Mr. Baumrind and the affects this has made? Can't sleep, lost thirty pounds in thirty days, can't eat, taking sleeping pills, can't work, it's really hard on him. And, the good doctor says, well, Vernon's not getting what he's paying for. You've just inconvenienced him a little bit. This guy's a real healer. I'm sorry I drew you apart. And I think about this man's poor wife. The poor unsuspecting woman that she is, the chattel. I feel sorry for her. There he is in the upstairs of his house talking to this gal on the phone while his poor wife is scrambling around trying to care for her kids, calling him to dinner and he's hanging on the telephone talking dirty to this lady in an effort to take her away from her husband. And he did it. He succeeded.

Ladies and Gentlemen, you know, I think it's ironic, they talk about my client being a "sicky" for sequestering himself secretly monitoring these filthy conversations. I think he's got a perfect right to be agitated and to be upset and to be here today. Let's talk about who is the "sicky." These fantasies over the telephone. Fantasies of what he, this doctor, got this lady doing for him that was distasteful to her, and she admits this to him. And, you talk about using women, preying on their emotions. It's like a meat market with this guy. He used his ex-wife. He used Mr. Baumrind's wife.

    The fact was that the marriage wasn't all that bad. And that was the truth. At one point in the tapes, he sounded surprised when he was talking to her and said to her, 'After I started seeing you, you told me it wasn't all that bad. Just sounded like you didn't want to get rid of him.' And, she responded, 'He has many good points, he's very understanding, he loves the children and tries so hard to be such a good father. He's been good to me.' The marriage got made bad deliberately for Dr. Ewing's personal benefit. Yes, there were problems, as there always are in marriages. But their problems got magnified by Dr. Ewing. Under his influence they became insurmountable by design. Going to his office, not for treatment, for something else. Marriage counseling? In his office when his office is closed to all others? In the park on a blanket? In her home in front of the fireplace, with the children within feet? Dr. Ewing used his professional knowledge, he used his training, he used his position as a treating physician on Mrs. Baumrind to gain her affections. He says, I tried to draw y'all apart. It's all there, and that's the truth of this case. The truth is in the innermost confines of these people's minds.

    Dr. Ewing's defense team is saying my client should have simply taken her back. There was no way to trust her. Who could trust somebody like this who was lying to him at every bend in the road? Truthfulness between two married people is important. If you don't have truthfulness, you don't have a marriage. This lady lied to him. She complains about him swooping in and taking the children. What was she and the good doctor planning to do? The doctor says he ought to have his keys to the house taken away so he can't just come and go. She says, yeah, we don't want to be interrupted when things are happening. The faster we get him out, the better. Does that sound like the woman he married?

These two people both traded up when they trashed their spouses. And their attorneys are here today telling you that Mr. Baumrind could have prevented all this. These two were sitting there planning all this for God only knows how long and they're saying he should have gone to Doctor Ewing and confronted him with all this. Ladies and Gentlemen, things don't work that way; and these lawyers sitting at that table with their client know this well. He was entitled to protect himself; to protect his children. This lady asked for alimony in the divorce-custody issue and was denied. She asked for a division of property, other than their house, and she was denied. She asked for a piece of his business, she was denied. It's all in there in the divorce decree. You've heard the evidence. I think my client has proven his case. He was perfectly correct in what he did. And I don't think an attack on him today as being the sick one who took his children is justified. I think he did the exact right thing in fighting for his children.

This doctor used psychological leverage to destroy that marriage. He got her to do things for him that were distasteful to her, and she admitted that to him, and yet he pursued her. He played on her emotions, manipulating her psychologically. He pursued her, knowing she was so imbued with him that she would do anything. Her emotional level, under his powerful influence distorted her value judgments. She got a taste of walking on the wild side, and he gave it to her. He knew he was giving it to her, and he kept saying things like, "Well, are you going to do it with Vernon one more time before you throw him out? I feel responsible. I tried to draw y'all apart." I submit to you that this is psychological.

But, he kept saying, yeah, you make up your own mind. I thought you thought of me all the time. That's what he told her. She says, 'Well, I was thinking so and so' and, he says, 'Well I thought you thought of me all the time?'

Mr. Foreman, we appreciate the attention you've given us. We appreciate the manner in which you've sat here for these five days. I'm sorry it has taken so long; but we're asking you for a fair verdict and your consideration which we know will be equitable."

The jury's verdict was rendered mid-afternoon of the final day of the trial in favor of the plaintiff with a $37,500 judgment: a shockingly low amount. It was learned several months later that one of the jurors had a connection with one of Ewing's three local attorneys. That was the major reason the Ewing team hired three attorneys: all local, each with a sphere of influence. The greater the number of local attorneys on board, the broader the base is from which to draw a more favorable jury; perhaps a juror who would be partial to one of the attorneys for some reason known only to the lawyer and the juror. That was the only disadvantage I had in having Jan Warner as my attorney, as Jan was from a distant South Carolina County and did not have the connections in Florence that he would have in his home county. We never did get a clear understanding of exactly what the Ewing connection with the juror was, but the foreman of the jury told Jan Warner several months later that except for this one juror they were all in favor of awarding the plaintiff $800,000. The single holdout told the others they could either agree to a $10,000 judgment or they may as well put in orders for their lunch for the next several weeks. After a five-day trial, on a Friday afternoon, the jurors simply wanted to get back to their normal lives. They "compromised" at $37,500 which was a miscarriage of justice.

CHAPTER EIGHTEEN

Ewing's behavior had proven to be habitual. Local, state, and national news coverage of the wiretap issue and alienation trial generated calls by former patients and employees of his to whom he had made advances in his medical offices or by phone following office visits. These women expressed an interest in supporting me primarily in future litigations to maintain custody and they encouraged me to ban with them in filing a complaint with the appropriate medical authorities. They were not willing to file complaints individually.

With the alienation trial concluded, I contacted the Medical Board of Examiners in the State of South Carolina about his conduct and provided contact information for each of these former patients who wanted to lodge complaints. Collectively, we were a force that could not be denied. In their investigations, the Medical Board identified several additional witnesses, and we all provided testimony at a hearing in Florence in 1983 in which the ultimate decision was to suspend his license to practice in the state. He had already lost his hospital privileges at the hospitals in Florence due to the bad publicity.

The South Carolina State Board of Medical Examiners rendered a "Final Order" in the James H. Ewing, M.D. case on September 19, 1986. Their Disciplinary Panel found the following acts of misconduct:

1. In February 1978, this doctor had unethical and unprofessional inquiries of and physical contact with an unnamed patient under his care, by improperly inquiring about her sexual habits and her sexual activities with her husband; and by touching her pelvic area in an unprofessional manner during her physical examination. The Panel found that during this time the doctor made unethical and unprofessional telephonic communications to this patient by making unsolicited telephone calls in which he attempted to get this patient to engage in sexual relations with him and to masturbate while talking with him on the telephone.
2. In April 1978, this doctor made similar unethical and unprofessional physical contact with and unethical and unprofessional telephonic communications to another patient. While in his office and after discussing the results of the examination with her, he purposely pressed his lower body against this patient in a fashion so that the patient was able to feel his erect penis. Following this office visit, he made unsolicited telephone calls to this patient and questioned her about her sexual habits and activities and tried to persuade her to masturbate while he was talking with her on the telephone. During this conversation, he told the patient he was himself engaging in masturbation. The Panel further found this doctor unethically and unprofessionally

had tried to persuade this patient to have sexual relations with him.

3. The Panel found that between July 1978 and August 1978, this doctor made unethical and unprofessional contact with a third patient by embracing her in the examination room of his office in a manner so that the patient could feel his erect penis. Thereafter, the doctor unethically and unprofessionally had intimate physical contact with this patient whom he knew was experiencing a deteriorating marriage.

4. The Panel found that between 1976 and 1978, while treating another patient, he made unethical and unprofessional telephonic communications to this patient, offering to teach the technique of masturbation while talking with her on the telephone. This offer was unsolicited and without a medical purpose.

5. The Panel found that during 1978, this doctor was affected by a mental condition that rendered further practice by him, at the time, dangerous to the public.

As a result of his misconduct, the State Board of Medical Examiners found that he had violated the Medical Code of Laws of South Carolina and they "suspended his Medical License and the privileges appurtenant thereto of James H. Ewing, M.D. for an indefinite period but that suspension" was immediately stayed, and he was placed on a period of indefinite probation during which time he was required to report to the Medical Board every six months. He was to strictly comply with Medical Practice Laws of

South Carolina and the Rules and Regulations of the Board. A violation of the terms of the probation would result in the immediate imposition of the indefinite suspension of the doctor's medical license and privileges.

Ewing appealed the Medical Board's findings to the South Carolina Supreme Court and as part of his appeal, he asserted that the Board should be enjoined from publishing its findings of fact and conclusions of law in its final order. The Supreme Court cited cases to the contrary, rejected his appeal and asserted their opinion that after reviewing the complete record of the case, "we readily agree" with the findings.

In other incidences reported, former employees of his disclosed that, because of advances made to them in the office, the employees had agreement between themselves that they would never leave just a single employee alone in the office with him at any one time. It was revealed that he would often be noticeably erect in the office. At least one employee who was approached improperly by Ewing personally indicated she had asked the doctor if he did this "with every employee," and that he had responded, "Just the special ones." The same was reported by one of the former patients who asked the same question, "Do you do this with all your patients," with the identical response, "Just the special ones."

The Oprah Winfrey Show, a daytime syndicated talk show that aired nationally for 25 seasons, the highest rated talk show in American television history, contacted me one morning in late 1986 asking me to fly to and from Chicago for an appearance the next day with Oprah for a discussion about wiretapping cases that were cropping up across the country as a result of the Baumrind vs Ewing case. It was not the thing for me to do at the time; and I graciously declined the invitation.

ABC News filed suit against the Florence County Clerk of Court in an attempt to secure access to the Baumrind divorce-custody files which had been sealed by the family court judge in April 1979. The records had been unsealed prior to the Baumrind vs Ewing suit in order to give the Ewing attorneys access to them. The alienation trial judge ordered the records resealed after the conclusion of trial, ruling that "no public purpose can be served by invading the sanctity of the marital relations of these parties. To do so would serve only the prurient interest of the bizarre and macabre and surely could not be of public interest."

ABC's 20/20 syndicated TV program, with Hugh Downs and Barbara Walters, along with correspondent John Stossel pursued access to the sealed family court documents unsuccessfully for several years until eventually on July 18, 1985, they aired a segment entitled, "Is Someone Listening," a segment on being electronically bugged, "often by people we know and trust." Hugh Downs commented, "The last thing we expect when talking to a friend or a coworker is that our conversation is being secretly recorded. Privacy is sacred to us. We fight to protect it, and we expect privacy."

"But in a surprising and disturbing report, consumer correspondent John Stossel tells us that our privacy can be invaded, and our conversations bugged in unexpected ways and unlikely places by people we least suspect." John Stossel reported, "When I think of wiretapping, I think of governments wiretapping one another…But tonight, we're not going to be talking about the government or professionals, because it turns out that bugging in this country is being done by people like you and me…take for example, the case of wiretapper Vernon Baumrind in South Carolina…who began to suspect his wife of eleven years was having an affair with her doctor, James Ewing. He'd come home and find her talking on the telephone in low tones, and sometimes hanging up the phone quickly as he entered the house." It was explained that "the Baumrind's had two children and custody was a major issue and that the wiretap was crucial in validating all that was occurring which had bearing on custody." Baumrind was asked, "Couldn't you have just confronted your wife? Why did you have to resort to a tape recorder?"

The response was that he "was up against a prominent doctor who would have more credibility than he would, and he would not have been believed had he not recorded these conversations. He says he was surprised at how easy it was."

The essence of the program aired was about the rights of the people being bugged. Is this legal? Well, the answer is both "yes" and "no." John Stossel pointed out that Presidents Roosevelt, Truman, Kennedy, Johnson, and Nixon all had taped conversations in the Oval Office. Visitors may not have known they were being taped; but this was legal because one of the parties in the conversation, the president in this case, knew it was being recorded. The law (at that time) basically acknowledged that this was legal when at least one of the parties' consents. But, as John Stossel pointed out, "What Vernon Baumrind did was different. Vernon was not part of the conversation. He was a third party, listening in on his wife and her lover. The Justice Department says third-party recording is a criminal act that carries both criminal and civil penalties as well as imprisonment for up to five years." Stossel further pointed out that the judge in Vernon's case cited a case in which wiretapping does not apply to husbands and wives, and the South Carolina State Supreme Court had ruled he was within his rights since the telephone was in his name, it was on wires within the confines of his home, and he was still living in the house where he tapped the phone. In fact, the doctor was not entitled to privacy within the confines of the Baumrind home. In other words, the legality of the wiretapping in this instance did not fall within "the legislative intent" of the law.

It was stressed that how the interception of conversations is accomplished is pertinent; that a violation would have occurred if the husband had entered his estranged wife's home and placed a recording device on her telephone that intercepted conversations between the wife and her lover. The husband would be clearly in violation. Even though the South Carolina Supreme Court ruled that interspousal wiretapping between spouses who live together is beyond the scope of the law (Baumrind v. Ewing, 276 S.C. 350, 279 S.E.2d 359 (1981), had the parties been estranged or had one of them used a private investigator to accomplish the surveillance, the court may have reached a different result. Baumrind's lawyer was interviewed and advised "not to try it…that Vernon was lucky; today people are being prosecuted for this." John Stossel directed a question to the public: "Would you want this done to you?"

Stossel also pointed out that after the Baumrind trial, a lot of people nationwide started bugging each other. Many lawyers were unaware of the legal liabilities implicated when an individual uses electronic surveillance to spy on his or her spouse (interspousal wiretapping), and subsequent rulings by various courts were mixed. Radio Shack (Tandy Corporation) was sued in 1981 for selling telephone taping devices to suspicious spouses who used them based on the Baumrind decision to bug home phones for evidence they could take to divorce court.

DECEIT

The Charlotte Observer published an article discussing wiretapping at the time:

> It was noted that the "state security manager for Southern Bell Telephone had blamed the court decision in the Baumrind matter for a significant increase in suspected wiretapping complaints and inquiries with the company as to legalities of recording phone calls in this manner." The security manager stated, "The increase in wiretapping cases is alarming, considering there is a federal law against it and that innocent third parties are often recorded and being damaged. Our customers have an expectation of privacy, and this is serious." In 1982, the company received hundreds of complaints and found recording equipment which was confiscated. The posture of the telephone company was that the Supreme Court "should change its position in the Baumrind decision; that it was, indeed, a very unfortunate decision rendered by the State Supreme Court."*

---

* THE CHARLOTTE OBSERVER, Tuesday, February 8, 1983, "Marital Wiretap Cases Cropping Up In S.C. Courts," by David Reed, Associated Press:

CHAPTER NINETEEN

EWING

Like the proverbial "kid in a candy store" who grows up to be a chocoholic working on a Hershey's factory assembly line, James Ewing, no doubt aware of his sexual appetite in his 20's, navigated his way into the dream career for a sex addict - a gynecologist. As a "doctor," typically revered, this lofty platform afforded Ewing a huge advantage, gaining him access to and status over a plethora of women and personal information that a typical sex addict doesn't have. His practice was a mere playground for himself. And, as revealed by patients and former employees who stepped forward, he repeatedly used that power to leverage himself with patients and employees for purposes having nothing to do with the typical reasons a woman visits her gynecologist. He could prey upon unsuspecting and vulnerable women who would succumb to his power and influence. His medical degree was nothing more than a hunting license. In his private domain, he could sidestep convention to exploit his status as a doctor in highly unethical fashion. He was able to do this with immunity, until Baumrind vs Ewing.

In the early 1980s there was no information available on bad doctors as there is now. Today hospitals and other medical employment agencies can research the backgrounds on doctors seeking employment. The US Congress passed a Health Care Quality Improvement Act in 1986 establishing a National Practitioner Data Bank (NPDB) which created a repository of data on incompetent, negligent and disciplined doctors. Prior to this time, medical practitioners were able to move freely between states, with state licensing boards and hospitals largely unable to learn of lawsuits, disciplinary proceedings, and other actions in other localities that may have otherwise flagged bad doctors.

Following the alienation trial, as related previously, Ewing lost his hospital privileges in Florence, South Carolina and was forced to seek employment elsewhere. He and Linda initially relocated from Florence to Wadesboro, North Carolina. However, several years later he was released from employment there when his past caught up with him. They relocated again to Alderson, West Virginia for a job as the resident gynecologist at the Alderson Federal Prison Camp for Women, a minimum-security prison where the TV icon and cookbook legend, Martha Stewart, was later incarcerated in 2004 after her conviction for financial crimes. The Ewings lived on the grounds of the Penitentiary for several years. When his past record was discovered, his employment was again terminated. From there, they moved to Utica, New York and, later, relocated again to Mississippi. Ultimately, they moved back to Columbia, South Carolina. Early in his professional career Ewing had a pharmaceutical license before becoming a gynecologist. In Columbia, he reacquired his pharmaceutical license and gained employment at a local CVS pharmacy until his retirement. This late occupational changeover is inexplicable to all but himself and, perhaps, his current wife, Linda.

Fortunately in this country, generally, we have a fair and effective justice system that has protections built into it to preserve the rights of individuals; however, sometimes, as in the case of the Ewing matter, there are loopholes in the system that allow the guilty to slip through and escape justice and that appears to be what happened in this case wherein the Medical Board was not able to get a complete picture of his misdeeds. As a consequence, he was able to move continuously from place to place until his reputation caught up with him in those locations; presuming similar incidents to those in his past had not surfaced as well.

In the end, his wife Louise divorced him. His only daughter, Victoria, has been estranged from her father for more than 20 years and hasn't allowed her children around him. His only son, Wade, took his own life in his early twenties in the aftermath of all the litigations and bad publicity at the time. We were all innocent victims of Ewing's sex addiction and his unethical behavior, and our lives were devastated by this man. His son's devastation was fatal.

LINDA

While initially it was Ewing's sex addiction alone that was the catalyst for their adulterous relationship, what is not known for certain is whether Linda, herself, over time became an addict. He obviously got her started on the path of sex obsession to compulsion, like himself, with the need for frequent sex in one form or another with or without a partner. Did she, too, become an addict? How could she not; while living with and accommodating him all these years now? Could her addiction to sex be the reason she could not come back to her family? That revelation, if true, would certainly validate the importance of the outcome in the custody issue. As well, it may even answer anyone's question as to how she could give up her children for a man with his history; especially after his disreputable lifestyle became well-known to her.

Ultimately, oblivious to this man's motives, which should have been obvious to her early on, coupled by her own character defects, she made it possible for the disastrous series of events and consequences to occur. If she had been contrite even once in the slightest fashion, I would have been equally willing to consider forgiveness; but only to the extent of her contriteness. But she never was! Except for a couple of lame attempts at getting me to bend, all I experienced was arrogance and negativity. To this day, she remains defiant. She has never had the grace to apologize to our children, now adults, for the sadness and disruption she caused in their lives. She insists that what happened is "no one's business," and she won't discuss any aspect of it with them. I think it is their business, frankly! But I'm only saying so in this writing, as for all these years I have been very careful not to say anything negative of my children's mother to them or to say anything that would create conflict between them and her or put them in the middle of any controversy between her or me. This book may change that.

I always tried to counter her negativism with the positive; always trying to demonstrate that there are alternative ways to see the same issue. As little children, David and Jade would return from weekend visits with their mother and tell me, "Daddy, Momma hates you." I would tell them, "I'm sorry she feels that way. I will always love her for what we shared together, especially for you," with a big hug and a kiss.

As humans, everything we do - our actions, words, and choices, our accomplishments and goals, our purpose, how we use our time, how we treat one another, the compassion we feel and the kindness we demonstrate, even our failures, deficiencies, and bad deeds—all determine the mark we leave on posterity—our legacy. The words of Maximus Decimus Meridius, "…What we do in life…echoes in eternity," resonate in my mind with great weight and truth.

When I think about Linda these days, I like to ponder the girl and woman I knew for 12½ years. Everything about her made her a dream fulfilled: the love of my life from the moment I laid eyes on her to our first kiss to excitedly marrying her to years of success together to the birth of two amazing children and our dream home. Her respect for elders, the gregarious way she had with friends and older folks, her sweet, demure disposition, and her stunning physical beauty made Linda a true dream-come-true. Outwardly and inwardly she was simply captivating as she took my breath away every day. She inspired me with love I had only heard in music. The most profound level of love I could ever imagine since I was a boy was the one I was living! A high-bar had been set with Linda which was never matched thereafter. I was unwilling to ever settle for anything less than I knew I had with her. Instead, I've chosen gratitude for the joy and peace of our 12½ good years together.

UNDERSTANDING WHAT HAPPENED

As tragic as these events were in the lives of our family, the opportunity to understand what happened and how it was possible to happen is a good thing and provides some degree of closure. The writing of this story required the consideration of all the facts and events for the first time in total, years later. This has brought to light revelations that were not apparent early in the actions that were adjudicated individually some forty-five years ago before all the facts were known in the custody issue, the alienation trial and in Medical Board actions.

For example, at the time of the initial child custody hearing and the alienation trial, the testimonies of James Ewing's multiple victims and the eventual results of the South Carolina Medical Board findings were not available. These testimonies and findings had not yet all been revealed, nor had the findings been determined. Additionally, the South Carolina Medical Board of Examiners had missed the severity of the mental condition of Dr. Ewing - not altogether their fault. The sealing of the Baumrind files by the Florence County Clerk of Court prevented the full disclosure of those facts. Had the Medical Board had access to the content of the wiretapped conversations of the doctor, they too may have had a different opinion as to the severity of his mental condition. His addiction to sex would certainly have been obvious; an affliction that would render him dangerous to his patients. Additional adverse testimonies that surfaced after the principal litigations—those of Ewing's employees—were not available at the time of the Medical Board proceedings either. It's not known why the Medical Board did not consider the facts of the Baumrind case, but there was no mention of those facts in the Medical Board misconduct findings. The rulings in the Medical Board order only specified incidences relating to a few select patients. As a result, the Medical Board conclusions were a miscarriage of justice. This allowed him to thwart the system and to continue practicing gynecology in his demented state to retirement.

Collectively, any one of the events including hearings, trials, and Medical Board findings, may have had different results had all the evidence conjointly been available at critical times. The content of the taped telephone conversations, the patient and employee sexual assault testimonies, and the publication of the Medical Board conclusions, in their totality with the writing of this story make it evident that the physiological drive this doctor had for anything carnal was overpowering due to his addiction to sex manifesting itself with multiple women and pornography. His appetite for sex in any form was insatiable. He was in a desperate state to obtain more of it and more frequently in one form or another. This is seen in his obsessive conversational behavior brimming with sexual innuendos, references, cravings, and brash pronouncements, and in his compulsive actions to obtain sex either with a partner, whomever that may have been, or by self-manipulation or both. He had poor-to-no boundaries, poor social skills, and a poor ability to interact with family and others, some of whom found him creepy in their interactions and were not comfortable around him. Over his lifetime, there may not have been a single person close to this man who was not negatively affected in one way or the other.

All the pieces of this puzzle have come together all these years later and, more recently, have been confirmed by family members, who report he creepily stares at them from the corner of his eye or across the room with an intensity that makes them feel uncomfortable. Is it the "creep stare" of one who is attracted to you, but can't do anything about it? One can only contemplate. Does this stare emanate from an insecurity within himself which is expressed to a female he wants, but can't have? Or is it the overconfident, arrogant "Bad Boy" rising up figuratively since he can't literally? They sense something is a little (or a lot) "off," but they can't pinpoint the issue. They sense it. Their intuitions tell them something is wrong. But they don't know this story that I, and now you, know.

Currently, the weight of the evidence altogether provides the answer to what happened and how these events occurred—all of which the psychiatrists, the family court judge in the custody hearings, the witness testimonies and jury conclusions at the alienation trial, and the Medical Board of Examiners missed early on, allowing this doctor to continue practicing gynecology unhinged for years to retirement. Even the one and only great attorney, Jan Warner, missed this revelation, which if he had not, may well have resulted in a much more favorable outcome in the alienation trial; but, maybe not with the biased juror.

AND THE VERY REASON THIS STORY MUST BE TOLD

As indicated, the cumulative knowledge today of everything that happened, and the writing of this story raises awareness that these things can happen—that they do happen—and will continue to happen to others when people, like Dr. James H. Ewing, have a pathway into your life. It was the pathway that Linda provided for him. She made it all possible. Assuredly, these things have happened to others untold times in the interim since 1978-79, without the advantage of wiretap technology. Undoubtedly, the elements of this chronicle have been repeated and are already in process again, now, somewhere else by others, like James Ewing, to some other unsuspecting family, with similar devastating results in wait. Gaining an awareness, the vision of the possibility of this series of events happening in one's life, may be the most important benefit to be derived from this narrative account, and the very reason this story must be told. For me to take this story to my grave would be derelict, irresponsible and an injustice to my fellow man. I have already waited too long for many to benefit by my having postponed the telling of this tale. It would be a travesty for humanity for this story to be kept under wraps, where it has been for all these many years now, and to go untold. It has been my obligation to tell this story.

As painful as it has been to relate these details and as uncomfortable as it has been to disclose the indecent content, there is much to be learned from all that occurred, and I have shared these facts in hopes of enlightening, empowering and forewarning others of the ill effects of self-absorption. But now, of course, with the revelation of all the details, we know that it was much more than just two narcissistic people absorbed in themselves. It was much more complex than just that. There was the pervasion of an overpowering, inescapable and undeniable element of sex addiction in the miscreant character of James Ewing at play that drove this narrative forward. And, beyond that, by her acquiescence to him, Linda made it possible for all the damage that was done and the pain inflicted on her family that lingers to this day.

Ultimately, this account accentuates the fact that sometimes people of great esteem, including professionals highly regarded in society, are deficient in character and morals and are, themselves, the perpetrators of serious improprieties. Their lofty positions of authority often provide cover and opportunity for abuse and exploitation. They often feel exempt from accountability and retribution. As in the case of the unethical doctor in this story, whose personal character was catastrophically flawed, he was controlling, domineering, and manipulative, with an attitude of entitlement. The most powerful element at play in the events related was this doctor's overriding power and influence which he used to advantage himself to the detriment of everyone in his life.

To combat this kind of harmful behavior from anyone, one must first recognize the conduct for what it is and, then, have the fortitude to resist it. The disclosure of the details of this story serves to illustrate the devastation that occurs when there is no resistance to conduct like this doctor's.

I hope this story will be enlightening and empowering to those who may be experiencing similar events and feeling helpless. Even if the only take-away is an awareness that these things can and do happen, that they can happen to anyone, that no one is immune, that one should not be naïve enough to think this is not a possibility in their life, the writing of this story will have served its purpose. To those reading this tale who have a marked propensity to act as the antagonists herein acted, this book may serve to give pause for reflection on the myriad and immeasurable negative consequences of irresponsible and thoughtless actions like those of the two antagonists. If the story prompts one predator, like the doctor in this account, to avoid behavior as destructive as related herein, this account will have been worth writing. If this story enlightens and empowers one person, like my wife in this account, to resist such behavior as hers, this narrative will have been worth recording. This is especially true as these actions directly affect the ones in our lives we should love and value most: our families. For those who have not had to go through anything like this, I hope this story is illuminating and provides a greater appreciation for and commitment to the bonds of love that currently exist in your life.

It is my profound hope that by sharing these explicit details, some other family may be able to avoid a similar tragedy. Knowledge gives us power to exert some control in our lives. Just being aware that such things as these reported herein are possible is powerful to know. Having knowledge enables us to make wiser decisions; to avoid dangers which can consume us—and those we love. This is the ultimate benefit of this writing I hope will be well-received. As in all aspects of humanity where progress can be made, the replication of mistakes must be avoided. Continuing to conceal the knowledge of this story would be a travesty unto itself - lessons learned would be gone to waste. There must be some good that can come from the disclosure of all these details, and that is my eternal hope in the writing of these events. Awareness is power!

THE GIFTS: THE CHILDREN

More than anything else in the lives of my children, I wanted to instill in them the best qualities of character including the virtues of kindness, consideration, understanding, sympathy, tolerance, respect, morality, integrity, ethics, dignity, honesty, and compassion. These admirable traits were devoid in the characters of both antagonists in this tale and I knew I'd be combatting and counteracting their mother's influence as the children grew up. I almost lost that chance. I'm delighted to report: Mission Accomplished! There is no greater reward in my life.

All worked out best for us. The children grew up as wholesome, highly principled adults with undeniable grace and dignity, and I did not have to live with a wife who could not return my love. My greatest sense of accomplishment today in all these years is in the exemplary characters of my children and my grandchildren who learned well from their parents whose virtuous qualities they chose to reflect. My children and their children are aware of the disparity in the characters and the lifestyles of their grandparents, and they often speak of this. I am grateful that they have the ability to distinguish the differences. As it is, I have been very successful and blessed. By contrast, if I had not taken the action that I did, for certain, the children would be different people today; not for the better. Even they recognize this, as they have stated their good fortune for the way things turned out, under all the circumstances.

GRATEFUL ME

While the loss of my intact family has been the source of sorrow to which nothing has compared, I am filled with gratitude for the fortune that I did have. I had the privilege and pleasure of raising my two children. My son, daughter and four grandchildren are blessings too rich to describe in words. I am incredibly proud of each of them. My business ventures have been rewarding. I've had a full, eventful life otherwise with pleasure from diverse activities that have kept me busy and productive every day. I enjoy great health. At 78 I'm playing tennis every other day with guys 10 years younger than I am. Yes, there has been a void in my life with the loss of the wife with whom I had dreamed I would share joys, challenges, and triumphs of life. Since then I've been unable to match the measure of love I had for Linda during those years together and, knowing how special that love was for me, I found myself unwilling to compromise for less. The emptiness still hurts on a level no one can ever understand. But, that void motivates me now to do what I can to help others become aware and avoid similar circumstances as those related herein. For this reason I've written this account; and I hope that, perhaps, an even greater good than what I have realized in my life will emerge from the pages of this book.

FINALE

In the end, from a tenuous beginning, by controlling my emotions, containing my impulses and concealing what I knew, and by sheer perseverance, I was able to obtain custody of the children and responsibility for their lives. I had been as deceptive as she and he were, and my deception enabled us to get so far ahead of them that they were never able to catch up to us. I had matched their deceit with my own, and my deceit prevailed.

AUTHOR BIO

Vernon Baumrind is the father of two adult children and grandfather of four, living in Charlotte, North Carolina. Vernon is a successful businessman. He holds a patent on a unique recycling technology and the copyright on this story. He is 78 years of age.

To communicate with the author, please use the "Contact Form" in the website,
DeceitTheBook.com.

Made in United States
North Haven, CT
26 August 2024